The Empires' Edge

The Empires' Edge

MILITARIZATION, RESISTANCE, AND TRANSCENDING HEGEMONY IN THE PACIFIC

SASHA DAVIS

THE UNIVERSITY OF GEORGIA PRESS
Athens and London

Athens, Georgia 30602
www.ugapress.org

Set in 10/13 Minion Pro
Printed and bound by Thomson-Shore, Inc.
The paper in this book meets the guidelines for permanence and durability of the Committee on Production Guidelines for Book Longevity of the Council on Library Resources.

Most University of Georgia Press titles are available from popular e-book vendors.

Printed in the United States of America
18 17 16 15 14 P 5 4 3 2 1

Library of Congress Cataloging-in-Publication Data

Davis, Sasha, 1971–
The empires' edge : militarization, resistance, and transcending hegemony in the Pacific / Sasha Davis.
pages cm. — (Geographies of justice and social transformation)
Includes bibliographical references and index.
ISBN 978-0-8203-4456-0 (hardcover : alkaline paper) —
ISBN 0-8203-4456-7 (hardcover : alkaline paper) —
ISBN 978-0-8203-4735-6 (paperback : alkaline paper) —
ISBN 0-8203-4735-3 (paperback : alkaline paper)
1. Islands of the Pacific—Relations—Developed countries. 2. Developed countries—Relations—Islands of the Pacific. 3. Hegemony. 4. Militarism—Islands of the Pacific. 5. Militarism—Environmental aspects—Islands of the Pacific. 6. International cooperation—Philosophy. 7. Geopolitics—Islands of the Pacific. 8. Social movements—Islands of the Pacific. 9. Islands of the Pacific—Politics and government. 10. Islands of the Pacific—Environmental conditions. I. Title.
DU68.D48D38 2015
355'.033095—dc23

2014015866

British Library Cataloging-in-Publication Data available

CONTENTS

ACKNOWLEDGMENTS

Putting together a book is a group project. It feels almost absurd that only one name appears on a book given the tremendous support, inspiration, and help required to make it become real. This book, the result of over a decade of researching and writing, would not exist if not for the contributions of so many people it is difficult to give an exhaustive listing. I will try to give credit to the major players, but (in typical rhizomatous fashion) I cannot easily figure out any end to the sources that enabled this book to come to be. From my family to colleagues to people who took part in interviews to the theorists I read, this book has been shaped by the insights and generosity of many people.

More centrally to the production of this book, however, I need to recognize that without my interview respondents (who shall remain anonymous) and the people who helped me set up those interviews, this project would never have begun. I thank the many people around the world who have been generous of their time, sharing the concerns of their communities and introducing me to many of the people I interviewed for this research. I am particularly indebted to Nilda Medina, Robert Rabin, Michael Bevacqua, Kyle Kajihiro, Terri Keko'olani, Hinton Johnson, Jack Niedenthal, Hope Cristobal, Shinako Oyakawa, Yukari Akamine, and Yoko Fujita. I also want to thank my academic mentors: Tom Paradis, Alan Lew, Nancy Lewis, James McCarthy, Lakshman Yapa, Roger Downs, and Duarte Morais. I want to send a particular thanks to my dissertation advisor and mentor, Lorraine Dowler, who encouraged me to not shy away from the big issues in the world. She encouraged me to follow this line of research and throw caution (and travel budgets) to the wind in pursuit of what is important. She has been a role model and an inspiration.

Some parts of this manuscript have appeared as articles and so have been greatly enhanced by numerous rounds of helpful critique and revision. I want to specifically thank Jessica Hayes-Conroy for her collaboration on parts of this research and her support as a fellow researcher and friend over the course of this project. I also want to thank Allison Hayes-Conroy, who has seen this book in all phases of its development and has also given me helpful feedback. This book's arguments have also been made stronger by numerous anonymous reviewers and by particularly helpful comments from Jenna Loyd and Koohan Paik. I also want to thank the editors at the University of Georgia Press, Mick Gusinde-Duffy, Regan Huff, Beth Snead, Nick Heynen, and Deborah Cowen, for their help with the publication of this book—and especially Melissa Wright for suggesting that I contact the press for the project. All of the editors have been extremely helpful and supportive. I also want to thank Jennifer Comeau for her excellent work with the manuscript as well. I appreciate all the work everyone at the press has done to bring this book to publication. I also want to thank my colleagues at both the University of Vermont and the University of Hawai'i-Hilo for the support to allow me to conduct this research, particularly Glen Elder, Matt Hannah, Kathryn Besio, Sonia Juvik, Jim Juvik, Jon Price, and Dan Brown.

Lastly, I thank my family for their support and sacrifices as I wrote this book. My father, Frank Davis, has helped support me throughout the years of writing, and my mother, Susan Justice, deserves credit for turning my head toward issues of social justice for as long as I can remember. I also want to thank my kids—Sabine Maloney, Luca Davis, and Mariposa Davis—for their understanding when I had to hide in another room to type for hours at a time—but more importantly for also being sources of inspiration. I also thank Kathleen Kleman for her years of helping me with this project in ways too numerous to count. I also want to thank my love, Hillary Washburn, for her encouragement and for taking on so much as I completed this book. Without her, it certainly would have remained unwritten.

Sections of this book have appeared previously in the publications listed below. While much is revised, rearranged, and updated, some of the content is derived from these articles. I thank the reviewers and editors who helped shape some of the ideas that are in this final work.

Davis, J. S. (2005). Representing place: "Deserted isles" and the reproduction of Bikini Atoll. *Annals of the Association of American Geographers, 95*, 607–625.

Davis, J. S. (2007). Scales of Eden: Conservation and pristine devastation on Bikini Atoll. *Environment and Planning D: Society and Space, 25*, 213–235.

Davis, J. S. (2007). Military natures: Militarism and the environment. *GeoJournal, 69*(3), 131–134.

Davis, S. (2011). The U.S. military base network and contemporary colonialism: Power projection, resistance, and the quest for operational unilateralism. *Political Geography, 30*, 215–224.

Davis, S. (2012). Repeating islands of resistance: Redefining security in militarized landscapes. *Human Geography, 5*(1), 1–18.

The Empires' Edge

CHAPTER 1

Hegemony and Affinity in the Islands of Empire

The Asia-Pacific region has long been an important space between competing powers striving for economic and political dominance. Due to its status as a boundary area between great military powers, the Pacific hosts an astounding array of military bases, combat-training areas, weapons-testing sites, deployed naval vessels, and nuclear arsenals. In recent years it has become the focus of global military and diplomatic attention as North Korea tests nuclear weapons and missiles, China's economic and military strength grows, international disputes arise over small island groups in the East and South China Seas, and the United States pivots a majority of its military forces to the region. The Pacific region, however, is also something else. It is a homeland to the millions of people who live along its shores and inhabit the islands spread across the region. It is a region fragmented by colonial powers and caught between potent militaries, but it is also a region where countercurrents are gathering against "business-as-usual" militarized approaches to international security.

This book has two aims. First, using case studies from islands such as Hawai'i, Okinawa, Guam, the Northern Mariana Islands, the Marshall Islands, and the Philippines, it describes and analyzes the tremendous damage wrought on the people and environments of the Pacific region by American military activities—activities justified by the U.S. government's desire to maintain its global hegemony. Second, in an effort to relieve this region of the heavy toll of militarization, this book presents and promotes a perspective that rejects militarization, contemporary colonialism, and the idea that seeking hegemony is an inevitable condition of international politics.

Seeking Hegemony and Seeking Affinity in the Pacific

Most contemporary discussions of world politics take as a given that global politics is a realm of domination and submission where the only real question that needs to be asked is, "Who is going to dominate whom?" In practical terms this means that the great military and political game of the early twenty-first century is about whether the United States maintains its dominant role or gets challenged by its closest competitor, China. Central to this rhetoric of international politics is the idea of *hegemony*. While defined differently by numerous theorists, hegemony can be thought of as the domination of world affairs by one country over others (Kennedy, 1987; Wallerstein, 1999) or by the interests of one class over others (Gramsci, 1971). Hegemony is attained when competitors recognize the dominance of another power and acquiesce to its desires—or at least avoid open defiance against it. That dominance is attained not only through naked force or threats but also through favors and coercion. As the geographer John Agnew (2005) puts it, "Hegemony is the enrollment of others by convincing, cajoling, and coercing them that they should want what you want" (p. 2). Agnew also asserts that many individuals involved with international relations assume that the pursuit of hegemony and primacy in international politics is a given, "natural" state of affairs. In other words, the concept of hegemony has become so taken for granted that with no small amount of irony, the concept itself dominates other potential visions of conducting international relations. Geopolitical discourse includes the "hegemony of hegemony," wherein theories of how dominated groups can escape subjugation are generally limited to strategies in which the oppressed turn the tables, become dominant, and then participate in similar practices of domination for their own gain (Day, 2005).

A closer look at politics in the Pacific region, however, points to another alternative. In the space between the goliaths of the United States and China are thousands of islands whose inhabitants are caught in the middle of this global rivalry for hegemony. As a result, many of these islands are intensely militarized. Islands such as Okinawa, Guam, Jeju, the Hawaiian Islands, American Samoa, the Philippines, the Northern Mariana Islands, and the Marshall Islands are places where local environmental health and human security have been sacrificed for the sake of maintaining U.S. "national security" and hegemony in Asia (see maps 1 and 2). Something else, however, is also happening on these islands: social movements are rising and putting forward not just alternative, nonmilitarized visions for their colonized islands but also a different approach to geopolitics, an approach that challenges the premise that international relations must be framed by the logics of hegemony. Instead, these organizations are framing and practicing an agenda for international security based not on militarized systems of domination but on cross-ocean linkages of affinity and solidarity. Countering the militarization, and the drive for international hegemony that underpins it, these groups are constructing what I refer to as *affinity geopolitics*.

Affinity geopolitics is an approach to international relations where security does not require domination.[1] Instead of politics being a game of determining which group gets to enjoy security through achieving hegemony, affinity-based approaches borrow heavily from anarchist and feminist perspectives and insist that power can be deployed to destroy hierarchies and insider/outsider dichotomies, thereby bringing security to all. Groups engaging in affinity politics "are not oriented to allowing a particular group or movement to remake a nation-state or a world in its own image and are therefore of little use to those who seek power over others [hegemony], or those who would ask others for gifts, thereby enslaving themselves. Rather, they are appropriate to those who are striving to recover, establish or enhance their ability to determine the conditions of their own existence, while allowing and encouraging others to do the same" (Day, 2005, p. 13). In other words, the ethic underlying affinity politics is one of respect and mutual aid among communities and nations rather than one of domination, threats, and violence. Many of the antimilitarization and anticolonial social movements I discuss in this book demonstrate this kind of radical politics based on seeking affinity. I refer to these groups as practicing affinity geopolitics because they are operating not just at local scales but at regional and global scales as well (S. Davis, 2012). This deployment of affinity-oriented power in the borderlands between the Chinese and American military-economic-political spheres has the capability of throwing a more radical "third-way" possibility into geopolitical discussions about hegemony in the region (Soja, 1996).

It may be easy for politicians, strategists, pundits, military planners, geopolitical researchers, and theorists to overlook affinity-seeking groups from these small islands, but it is a mistake to do so for two reasons. First, through resistance to military plans, these groups are having substantial impacts on military operations in the region (particularly in Okinawa, Guam, and Hawai'i) and therefore on U.S. military capabilities and the geopolitical balance of power (S. Davis, 2011). Second, these groups are effectively offering an innovative approach to geopolitics while achieving environmental and human security for their communities. It is important to highlight this political force because, as feminist and anticapitalist scholars like Julie Graham and Katherine Gibson have emphasized (Gibson-Graham, 2008), political research is more powerful when it opens our imaginations to new political possibilities. I have therefore written this book not only as an account of what is happening in the region but also as a vision of what the region could be. By examining the operation of hegemony and affinity in the region, I hope this narrative can also inform debates and actions in other spaces and places. In short, while this is a book about the Asia-Pacific region, it is more fundamentally a book about power.

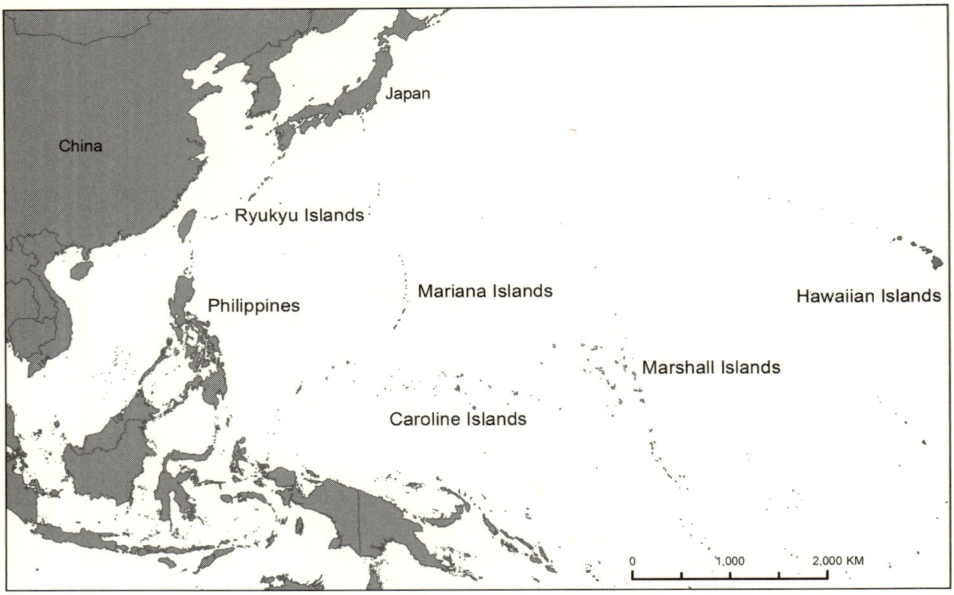

MAP 1. Island groups discussed in the book. Map by author.

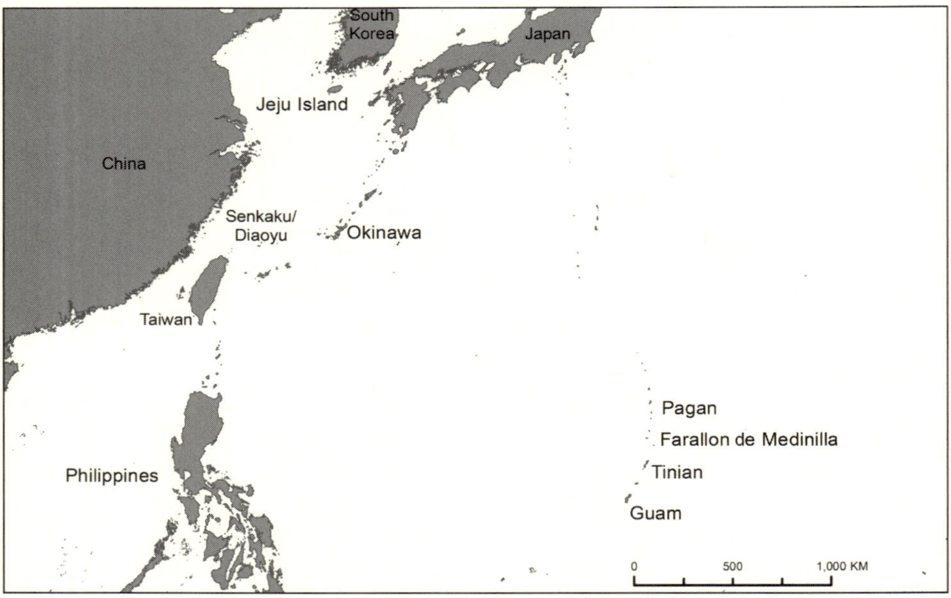

MAP 2. The Western Pacific with names of islands discussed in the book. Map by author.

Contemporary Geopolitics in Asia and the Pacific

The political scene in the Pacific has progressively become the foreign policy focus of government leaders in the United States in the second decade of the twenty-first century. Republicans, Democrats, military planners, conservative security analysts, weapons contractors, and think tanks have all increasingly represented this region as the new fulcrum of the global economy and the frontline of an invigorated geopolitical rivalry between the United States and an ascendant China (Clinton, 2011). While Hillary Clinton's 2011 piece in *Foreign Policy* is one example of this perspective, so is the report "Asian Alliances in the 21st Century" (Blumenthal, Mazza, Schriver, Stokes, & Russell Hsiao, 2011), released by the conservative American Enterprise Institute (AEI). Both paint the U.S.-China relationship as one of intense economic cooperation but also of likely political and military conflict. The AEI report assesses and measures Chinese armaments, imagines potential scenarios of conventional and nuclear combat, and calls for strong U.S.-led Asian alliances (with plenty of expensive American weapons systems). In the report one can also see the fingerprints of a very old geopolitical logic of hegemony in regard to the Asian "heartland," maritime "peripheries," and the importance of sea power that were made popular by British imperialist thinkers like Halford Mackinder (1904) more than a century ago. These ideas are still held by the contemporary theorists these military strategy papers repeatedly cite (like Posen, 2003). Many critical political and geographical theorists may no longer subscribe to the kinds of classical geopolitical perspectives embedded in the AEI report, but those discourses still have the power to shape political decisions (Ó Tuathail & Dalby, 1998). Many individuals in military and government institutions clearly still hold to these theories as well (L. Jones & Sage, 2010). As scholar of U.S. militarism Joseph Gerson notes, "[The American Enterprise Institute report] will certainly influence the policy options of Congressional Republicans and the Republican presidential aspirants, and of necessity reflects powerful trends of thinking within the Pentagon, and from first glance, it doesn't seem to be too far off what the Obama Administration is doing" (e-mail communication, 2011).

These think-tank reports and government pronouncements reveal a central paradox in U.S. policy toward China in the current century. China is one of the United States' most important trading partners and the top origin of imports into the U.S. economy. At the same time, the intense and increasing militarization of the Asia-Pacific region appears to denote an adversarial political relationship. This paradox makes more sense if we choose a different way to think about geopolitics, militarized security, and the positioning of military bases. Older conceptualizations of military power portray military bases as sites for defending the territories or regions in which they sit. This purpose for bases is no longer primary (and, as I describe more fully later, has never been the top priority in the Pacific). Instead, it is practical to think of bases as sites from which force can be projected and sites that ensure the functioning of critical economic and logistical processes.

To make sense of current U.S. policy in the Asia-Pacific region, the concept of "vital systems security" is helpful. Expanding on Michel Foucault's historical analysis of state power, Stephen Collier and Andrew Lakoff (2009) argue that states have deployed power for three reasons: state sovereignty, biopower, and vital systems security. They describe the history of state security apparatuses as initially being concerned with maintaining the state's territorial integrity and sovereignty. In other words, historically, states' primary concerns were defending territory and perpetuating the state against opposition. In time, however, states began to be concerned with surveilling and managing their own populations from the cradle to the grave. This birth of biopolitics entailed the regulation of public health, social programs, prisons, and the economy (Foucault, 2007). Collier and Lakoff (2009) add to these two concerns a third object of power: vital systems. These are systems or processes the state views as vital to its continued functioning and its ability to provide for its population. Examples include electrical power generation and transmission, fuel distribution, and the movements of goods (i.e., trade). Vital systems security is not divorced from other concerns of state power but integrated with them. For instance, states believe that a functioning electrical grid, transportation network, and so on help maintain a healthy population and maintain order that protects their territorial sovereignty.

The Pacific region is important to the American state today not so much because China or North Korea threatens U.S. territory or the well-being of the U.S. population but because the western Pacific is a critical space of a transnational economic system the American state feels it must protect. As Deborah Cowen (2010) comments, the American state views this area as a "logistics space" for trade that is critical for its very functioning. The U.S. position that trade with Asia is part of a vital system for the United States "transforms trade disruption from an economic cost to a security threat" (Cowen, 2010, p. 3). What is telling about this American political stance is that it displays in full glory the marriage of the American state with capitalist accumulation and neoliberal trade policies. U.S. foreign policy in the western Pacific essentially defines the continuation of free trade and capital accumulation (for companies favored by the U.S. state) as *necessary and vital* processes for the survival of the American state and nation. Furthermore, this policy is incredibly durable, having been in place for over a century with few substantial changes from one political administration to another.

As Agnew (2005) has pointed out, the processes of globalization (of which Asian trade is a staple) have an interesting historical relationship to the American state. The free-trade regime promoted by the United States since World War II led to globalization, "a hegemonic project intimately connected to the geopolitical calculus of the U.S. government and economic interests during the cold war" (Agnew, 2005, p. 2). The promotion of free trade and globalization was essentially the U.S. strategy to appeal to elites in other nations to support U.S. hegemony when it was challenged by the Soviet Union and China in the 1950s and 1960s. Though the economic regime of globalization, and specifically Asian trade, has taken on a life of its own that is not under the direct control of the American state, it is still the child of American political policies and therefore still viewed by the U.S. state as vital for its survival.

Looking at the Pacific region through the lens of vital systems security makes many of the apparent paradoxes and contradictions of U.S. foreign policy in the region more understandable. For instance, the U.S. military buildup in the region, while in some ways a balance to the increase in China's military capabilities, is less about being able to defeat China militarily (this is already possible) and more about leverage in dictating the terms of trade in the area. Also, when the U.S. government mentions that increased military presence in the area has to do with disaster relief, there may be a temptation to brush this claim off as an attempt to add humanitarian window dressing to military power so as to justify a larger presence of fighting forces. The claim makes sense, however, if one understands that military adversaries are not the only thing that can disrupt a vital system. Natural disasters, terrorist attacks, rogue state missile launches (i.e., North Korea), and technological failures are just as able to disrupt and challenge the security of Asian trade as an effective military adversary. Therefore, the U.S. military is present in this area to secure "the system" from all threats, environmental, military, and political. The rationale for continued U.S. political and military hegemony in the region is to be able to maintain this vital system.

Other states in the region see the system as vital as well. The governments of Japan, Taiwan, Singapore, the Philippines, Australia, South Korea, Thailand, and Vietnam have been recent supporters of U.S. hegemony in the region because those states, by and large, also view trade as a vital system for their countries. These states see the U.S. military as a force capable of protecting that system. Ironically, even some in China see it this way. China's position on militarily challenging the United States in the western Pacific is more complicated than it is sometimes portrayed in the American media and think-tank reports because

China, which holds U.S. debt and relies on exports for economic strength, has a strong economic motivation to avoid a military contest with the United States (Schweller & Pu, 2011). This ambivalence also explains why U.S. overtures for U.S.-Chinese military cooperation in the region make some sense even though each military is also maneuvering to contain and balance the other.

While many states may deem the western Pacific to be a space where a vital system needs U.S. military protection, the American military presence is also a politically thorny issue because the region falls outside the sovereign borders of the United States. The protection of networks and vital systems is sometimes hard to mesh with territorial logics of state power and traditional geopolitical conceptualizations of sovereignty (Harvey, 2003). Contemporary geopolitics, however, is focused not only on sovereign countries (or empires) jostling against one another but on the *interpenetration* of territorial sovereignty and networks of economic flows and power. As Hardt and Negri (2004) and Agnew (2005) point out, state power today is a hybrid of the network *and* territorial forms, a hybrid that includes states and other transnational entities as well. Agnew emphasizes that "this world has not been brought about predominantly through direct coercion or by territorial rule, but rather through socio-economic incorporation into practices and routines derivative of or compatible with those first developed in the United States" (p. 13). In other words, the vital system of Asian trade is a set of practices associated with capital accumulation and labor exploitation that may help the American state, but it no longer has a "homeland" per se. While viewing the system of trade as having no particular homeland gives credence to the idea that the system is the result of a hegemony of capitalist *practice* without any territorial hegemon (American or other), I endeavor to show in this book that the U.S. state still sees itself, and is still seen by other states and transnational corporations in the region, as the ultimate guarantor of that system. So while Agnew is explicit that the U.S. should be categorized as a "hegemon" supported by others as opposed to an "empire"—which connotes an international realm ruled by simple domination—I employ the term "American Empire" because it accurately depicts the role of the United States in the Pacific, even if the United States is influenced by other states and actors. After all, there are abundant recent examples of the United States behaving like an empire inside and outside the Pacific, especially since the attacks of September 11, 2001. After that date, U.S. policy began to veer sharply in the direction of protecting vital systems even if the policies and actions violated previously held conceptualizations of respect for the territorial sovereignty of other countries. The invasions of Afghanistan and Iraq were blatant examples, but so were cases such as the use of extraordinary rendition sites in nonsovereign "black holes" like Guantánamo Bay (Gregory, 2004; Hannah, 2006). In the case of the vital system of world trade, Cowen (2010) demonstrates how the post-9/11 American state has attempted to balance potential terrorist threats with the imperative of not slowing down trade by essentially extending American control to sites (particularly ports) that are in other nations' territory. These fine-scaled political colonialisms have been undertaken in the name of protecting vital systems.

On islands within the Pacific like Hawai'i, the Philippines, Guam, and American Samoa, however, this process is not a post-9/11 phenomenon: it has been going on consistently for over a century. Since at least the 1890s, the major concern of American power in the Pacific has been not to defend the island spaces from attack, and certainly not to provide and care for the populations that live on them, but to defend, protect, and steer the vital system of international trade with Asia. The islands that host military operations have been occupied and colonized not for direct economic gain through exploitation, but for their strategic positions from which the vital system can be secured. The reason many of these islands are *still* denied full sovereignty and subjected to intense militarization is because they are deemed to be critical for American "national security" (which in this region is essentially synonymous with American dominion over the vital system of trade).

This treatment of the island Pacific is legitimized by a particular geographical imaginary of Pacific islands as being unimportant and worthy of domination or destruction (J. S. Davis, 2005a; Gregory, 2004). As I investigate further in chapter 3, powerful myths circulate in policy circles, as well as in Western society at large, about what these islands are and what they are good for. As Melissa Wright (2006) has demonstrated, myths of disposability and worthlessness should not be taken lightly. These myths can serve as regulatory and policing mechanisms. They define what should be legitimate and limit what should be imagined and, therefore, limit what can be made real. They define the norms that legitimize actions—often very harsh and repressive actions. Furthermore, as social constructs, myths are difficult to counter because they operate by taking the results of cultural processes and recasting them as natural and socially unchallengeable "facts" (Agnew, 2009). Just as Wright demonstrated how transnational corporations have deployed the myth of female workers as disposable and lacking in value in order to extract value from them, place-myths of islands in the Pacific have been deployed to exploit islands for the American state's gain (J. S. Davis, 2005a; Shields, 1991; Wright, 2006). The value extracted from the islands I discuss in this book may not be directly related to commodity production, but they have obvious value in terms of power projection and the ability to control economic activities and direct capital flows. While the Pacific has millions of inhabitants, the region is often portrayed according to the myth of the "deserted island": as either an empty space or a space filled with islands that are uninhabited and insignificant (J. S. Davis, 2005a). This imaginary of Pacific islands allows outside powers to override local concerns and construct island landscapes as a marine borderland bristling with militarized fortifications and as a wasteland for projects deemed to be too environmentally damaging to perform closer to centers of power: nuclear weapons testing, missile defense development, and live-fire military training.

While a militarized borderland is one powerful geographical imaginary of the region, it is also a contested one. While myths may define norms, those norms can be challenged. "Normal" Pacific islands may be seen as too small to be allowed sovereignty or too critical to U.S. national security for local residents to make decisions about them, but resistance is widespread. People living in the Pacific have long challenged the idea of their islands as being useful "merely" to further outside agendas and protect systems of world trade that, for the most part, pass them by. Instead, islanders have been promoting a view of security that differs sharply from confrontational ideas of militarized national security and vital systems security (Aguon, 2006; Lutz, 2009; Women for Genuine Security, 2011). Over the past centuries, and continuing to today, people on islands such as Okinawa, Guam, Luzon, Jeju, Oʻahu, Tutuila, Tinian, and Kwajalein have produced geographical imaginaries that challenge outsider narratives about what the islands should be used for. This project of reimagining the region should not be taken lightly. Challenging and destroying myths is not just a poetic or cultural nicety; it is a vital political project. If new futures are to be imagined and made real, old myths about the region must be buried and new myths proposed (Hauʻofa, 1994; Shigematsu & Camacho, 2010; Wilson, 2000).

In this book, I focus on the ways people in these colonized and militarized spaces *within* the Asia-Pacific region define their places—and the effects these imaginings have. Traditional perspectives on power politics in the region may rest on questions of hegemony (Can the United States keep it? Will China get it?), but I explore a different realm of geopolitics in the region by focusing not on how power is applied to the region from outside, but on how it is being contested from within the Pacific. I argue that what is at stake today in the region is not just who gets hegemony or control over the vital system of Asian trade. Rather, what is being contested is whether hegemony and domination, as practices, can be *transcended*—not just in the Pacific region, but beyond. The islands of the Pacific are more than merely the stage where faraway capitals (and capital) play out dreams of hegemony. They are also the places where political ideas are emerging that challenge not only imperial powers, but the very notion that international relations must be arranged in relationships of hegemony and submission. Individuals and social movements are emerging, and networking across the region, that demand different ways of defining peace, security, and political relationships as based on solidarity, affinity, and mutual aid rather than on domination. It is not a coincidence that the sites of these new social movements are the places that bear the heaviest burdens of the imperial ambitions of distant powers, particularly the United States. As I will detail, the Asia-Pacific is a region of large militaries, enormous economic flows, and grand geopolitical designs and contests. The region, however, is also a place where militarism, globalization, and empire are being effectively contested and resisted.

The Empires' Edge

To describe the situation in the contemporary Pacific I attach multiple meanings to the book's title: *Empires' Edge*. In a descriptive geographic sense, the Asia-Pacific region—particularly the sites I focus on—can be seen historically as the edge of not just the American Empire but also the Chinese, Russian, Japanese, British, French, and Spanish Empires (with the Dutch and Portuguese at times in the mix too). For this reason I place the apostrophe after the "s" in the title. The Pacific has been and continues to be a place where the realms of *multiple* powers have met and pushed against each other. It is where Chinese power has jostled up against Japanese power, Japanese power against Russian power, and American power against Spanish, Japanese, Russian, and Chinese power. It is a region with a history of being the stage for the imperial adventures of others as well as the well-armed periphery that defines the edges between the realms of various powerful expansionist states.

While this region may be an edge or periphery to great powers, it is, of course, the center for people who live there. As scholars, particularly from the postcolonial perspective, have pointed out, margins and borderlands have been dynamic and fruitful places to find innovative ideas and practices that challenge the standard operations of empires and the global capitalist economy (Peña, 1997; Wilson, 2000). In this book I endeavor to discursively "recenter" the region by focusing on what is happening *from within* the region as opposed to following the focus of external actors like think tanks and U.S. politicians who insist that the primary importance of the region's islands is as strategic "anchored aircraft carriers." My goal is to show that new ideas and practices can emerge from the cracks and spaces at the spatial edge of the empire.

I also deploy the term *Empires' Edge* in a hopeful, temporal sense. Some of the ideas and practices I focus on, the ones that resonate from these marginalized places, are designed to contest not just one empire or another, but the underlying practices and ideas that legitimize and reproduce empires *in general*. In this sense, the term helps argue that we may be reaching the end of the epoch of great empires. While the traditional powers are scrambling to position themselves in the region to enhance and prolong regional and global hegemony (the United States) or assert themselves as the heir to that hegemony (China), something is happening underfoot that seeks to transcend imperial methods of militarized geopolitics and hegemony-seeking power (regardless of which capital it emanates from) and replace it with a system of local self-determination and regional solidarity.

A world without empires, or an Asia-Pacific region filled with self-ruled rather than colonized islands, may sound like a utopian vision. I attempt to show, however, that the cracks in the foundations of American hegemony are easy to see in this region. The social movements and organizations furthering the anti-imperial vision are numerous and strong and have already accomplished important political victories. The power of these groups may not yet be dominant, but the groups have already taken some important steps that any group envisioning a radical or revolutionary change must take. Namely, they have already begun to imagine a postimperial world in the region and to devise strategies to gradually implement it.

Furthermore, if we take the literal meaning of the term *utopia* as a "no-place" ripped out of its historical, geographical, and cultural context, then the military planners, foreign policy strategists, and corporate managers who see the Pacific as a "blank slate" are the ones relying on an unstable utopian vision. Maintaining the militarized landscapes that implement this vision of the Pacific as a bastion of American power projection consumes astounding amounts of money, energy, goodwill, political clout, and human labor. Perhaps rather than asking whether a more peaceful and egalitarian future is possible in these militarized islands, we need to ask whether the far-flung and increasingly unaffordable network of military bases in the region can be sustained against rising popular discontent.

An important theme of this book is to demonstrate where the discontent in these militarized islands is coming from. It comes not just from an abstract ideological calculation that American imperialism is not as exceptional or benevolent as other forms of imperialism, or that Pax Americana's time has passed. It also comes from the day-to-day activities and practices of the U.S. military in the spaces of everyday living that are experienced by inhabitants as serious problems. The jet noise, the taking and holding of large tracts of valuable land, the chemical and radiological contamination, the perceived safety threats (from unexploded ordnance, training, or military personnel out for a night on the town), the incidents of sexual violence, the psychological burden of knowing that hosting bases makes their communities fair game as targets for nuclear or conventional retaliatory strikes: these are the everyday local-scale realities that spur political actions that "trickle up" to affect broad-scale national and global political landscapes.

People living in these islands are keenly aware of the irony that their communities, homes, environments, and bodies are made less secure in the name of providing national security for faraway others. Some phrase this awareness in positive terms: that they are willing and proud to make a sacrifice. Some frame it as an unjust and exploitative relationship. Regardless of how people in these communities view the acceptability of the burden, it is widely recognized as just that: a burden. In the remainder of this chapter my aim is to set the stage for discussing this burden by explaining my research approach and discussing perspectives on power that I employ throughout the book.

Research Approach

This book is based on research conducted from 2001 to 2013. I used various methods to conduct the research, but the foundation comes from visits to most of the sites discussed in the book. I predominantly used qualitative ethnographic methods such as participant observation and semistructured interviews, but I also analyzed government documents, maps, and remotely sensed images of the sites as well as activist and academic publication and writings. I performed interviews with residents, workers, military personnel, members of local governments, activists, scientists, visitors, and people working for a variety of U.S. government agencies during numerous visits to islands hosting American military outposts, weapons testing sites, and training areas. I conducted research during visits to the Marshall Islands (2001, 2002, and 2007), Guam (2007 and 2011), the Northern Mariana Islands (2007), Japan (2007), Okinawa (2011 and 2013), the Philippines (2011), and Hawai'i (where I have lived, worked, and visited in 1996–1997, 2003, 2007, 2009, and from 2010 to the present). Furthermore, additional research in Ecuador (2007) and Vieques, Puerto Rico (2005, 2006, and 2007), while not in the region, was instrumental for understanding the trajectory of the American Empire and the activities of resistance movements.

I am not a specialist on the Pacific region as much as I am an avid analyst of the American Empire, militarization, and social movements. I am not a child of the Pacific, but rather a Caucasian raised in Arizona, a state with its share of military bases and training ranges (not to mention proximity to the Nevada Nuclear Test Site, which was an active site of nuclear bomb tests throughout my childhood). I chose the sites for this book not for their location but for the processes occurring in them. I am interested in telling the story of contemporary colonialism, hegemony, and resistance in the region because these sites, while important in and of themselves, are also the sites of innovations in rethinking and deploying some basic political concepts.

While studying these processes, I have come to adopt the region as my home. I now write from a hybrid position of outsider/insider in the sense that I am resident in the region but not born of it. Also, I am resident in one small part of what is a truly vast region. I write this chapter from my home in Hilo on the "Big Island" of Hawai'i, which is very different from places like Guam, Okinawa, and Tinian Island but is also, in some ways, still emblematic of the region. It is a strikingly beautiful place with a history and present of colonial dispossession. My home is situated 55 kilometers from Pohakuloa Training Area, the largest DOD site in the islands, where frequent live-fire training has resulted in contamination from depleted uranium and other hazardous substances. Another 300 kilometers west of that lies O'ahu; close to a third of that island has been sealed off behind the fences of military installations. As I describe in this book, there is much that binds the islands of the Pacific together: similar landscapes, similar cultural heritages, and the ocean itself (Hau'ofa, 1994). Unfortunately, it is also bound together through its shared history of occupation, colonialism, and militarization.

To explain and situate my discussion of empire in the Pacific I rely on insights from several research traditions. I am a geographer by academic training, and much of my theoretical and methodological approach comes from that discipline. This is both useful and problematic since geography as a discipline has a long history of providing both support and criticism of imperialism (Kearns, 2004; N. Smith, 2003). Much of what I discuss in this book about the contest between systems of domination and systems of cross-border solidarity in the Pacific is based on very recent events and research. However, the theoretical currents that support both the present mainstream and radical perspectives on global geopolitics reach back in the discipline over a century. Concern with the spatiality of systems of global hegemony and affinity has a long history in geography. As Gerry Kearns (2004) argues, pivotal moments in early twentieth-century British geography essentially revolved around questions similar to what I am exploring in this book. Namely, should the discipline be directed toward a geopolitics of imperial hegemony that is useful to the state, as exemplified by Halford Mackinder's work, or should it be directed toward advocating for international networks of egalitarian affinity where "political frontiers are relics of a barbarous past," as argued by Mackinder's contemporary Peter Kropotkin (1885, cited in Kearns, 2004, p. 344)? I think it is fair to say that I join this long debate firmly on the side of Kropotkin's position.

Methodologically, I approach my research through the lens of human-environment interaction, endeavoring to understand how rhetoric and discourse, human behavior and activity, and the physical/built landscape operate as a mutually interacting triad (Lefebvre, 1991; Soja, 1996). I am particularly interested in how power functions in these realms. In other words, I am interested in why some people's views of particular places win out over others' when it comes to planning, management, and governance decisions. Put in a more theoretical way, I aim to explore not just how knowledges are positional and situated (Haraway, 1997) but also how those knowledges entwine with power to both perpetuate and destabilize hierarchies of power/knowledge (Foucault, 1980). For instance, on Guam, many Chamorro and other Guam residents consider the Pagat area in the northern part of the island to be a sacred space with ancestral remains and artifacts worthy of environmental protection. The military sees it as an ideal site for a live-fire training range. How do these differing visions of place drive contesting political projects, and how do these projects interact to make policies that legitimize the kind of landscapes that get constructed? Furthermore, how do these local contests reverberate across other scales to affect communities, human bodies, environments, and regional and global politics?

A fair criticism of foreign policy doctrine, and even much of the work in international relations scholarship, is that there is such a strong focus on the macro scale and on sovereign governments that currents in localities, non-governmental organizations, and social movements are not fully considered (Massey, 2004; Robinson, 1999; Shigematsu & Camacho, 2010; Sjoberg, 2008). For this book I have chosen to focus on these lesser-studied currents of resistance from a multiscalar perspective and to emphasize the activities and rhetorics of social movements that are forging a different political order in the region. Performing this kind of analysis requires examining scales from the global to the level of individual bodies. To understand militarization, colonial control, and resistance in the western Pacific I have drawn on critical global and regional-scale analyses of American militarism by authors such as the late Chalmers Johnson (2004, 2007), Andrew Bacevich (2003), Jim Glassman (2005), James Hentz (2004), and David Harvey (2003), but I have found that it is critical to supplement these analyses with finer-scale approaches from such research traditions as feminist geopolitics, political ecology, studies of social movements, and postcolonial studies. These traditions stress that "empire is in the details" (Lutz, 2006). To understand empire at the global scale, you must examine what is going on at other scales and pay close attention to political actors outside the realm of government policy makers, political consultants, and military planners (Bernazolli & Flint, 2009; Brown & Staeheli, 2003; Dowler & Sharp, 2001; Enloe, 1990, 2007; Flint, 2003; Gillem, 2007; Glassman, 2001; Hayes-Conroy & Hayes-Conroy, 2013; Herod & Wright, 2002; Hyndman, 2004; Lutz, 2006, 2009; Marston, 2000; Massey, 1991; McCarthy, 2005; Ó Tuathail, 1996; Seager, 1993; Shigematsu & Camacho, 2010; Vine, 2004). In other words, it is impossible to understand the politics of empire without understanding the places where it touches the ground and the bodies of people that reproduce and contest it.

Inspired by these theorists, I have chosen to approach a topic that is broad both geographically and conceptually—the environmental and social damage caused by imperial ambition and resistance to it in Asia and the Pacific—through a study of individuals and the small but critical islands that host the "Bases of Empire" (Lutz, 2009). By doing so I hope to demonstrate that the United States' position as global hegemon and a powerful player in Pacific and Asian politics is not as deterritorialized as some portray it (Agnew, 2005). Instead, American ability to project power in the region is dependent on places—politically contentious colonized places such as Okinawa, Guam, the Marshall Islands, the Philippines, and the Hawaiian Islands. These are places where the daily activities of the military cause problems in the spaces of everyday living. These problems are often framed as only local problems (environmental or health problems) or as the problems of individuals whom governments (and sometimes researchers) do not generally see as important geopolitical actors: women, children, people living in poverty, and the colonized. What I want to show is that these concerns are not less important than geopolitical concerns, but rather that they *are* geopolitical concerns. What research in feminist geopolitics and postcolonialism has done is to show that the production of foreign policy and national security also arises from these everyday spaces far from the centers of state power.

Furthermore, these actors and sites may also be sources of a political paradigm shift away from militarized views of "national security" and competing hegemonic empires to solidarity-based visions of security and mutual aid. One of the more exciting and empowering findings of the research focusing on formerly ignored scales and actors is the growing realization that power generated in these marginal geographical and social spaces can be of a *qualitatively* different nature than traditional political power. This is demonstrated through research on local activism where people in militarized spaces work to relocate the scale at which security is imagined away from "national security" to the scale of the community and the civilian body (Brown & Staeheli, 2003; Enloe, 1990, 2007; Hyndman, 2004; Kirk, 2008; Koopman, 2011; Lutz, 2006, 2009; Marston, 2000; Ó Tuathail, 1996; Seager, 1993; Women for Genuine Security, 2011). These researchers and activists have uncovered not only another source from which power can emanate, or other actors that can wield power, but potentially a power that operates differently and produces different material effects. Women's groups, indigenous people's groups, and antimilitarization groups are becoming powerful actors in the Pacific by deploying power based on the concept of affinity rather than hegemony. They are not just claiming a space for a Pacific-based power, but instead promoting a nonhierarchical approach to politics where security is defined not just at a different scale, or with differently placed centers, but in a different, nonmilitarized way.

Pacific movements, instead of engaging in a quixotic battle for hegemony against external great powers, have continued to strive to make hegemony less relevant through networked affinity and direct resistance to the militarization of their communities. Put another way, power operates in the region in more than one way. I refer to the different methods of deploying power as hegemony-*seeking* and affinity-*seeking* to emphasize that hegemony and affinity are never closed projects. Hegemony—whether at the level of countries, classes, or the realm of ideas—is never total. There is always some form of resistance working against it, and there are always spheres in which domination has not yet been achieved (Gramsci, 1971). Likewise, affinity is never a completed project. There are always other "others" with whom an individual or group has not yet formed a bond of solidarity (Day, 2005).

Hegemony-Seeking Power

Hegemony-seeking power is based on exclusion and domination (i.e., inside vs. outside groups, citizens vs. aliens, colonizer vs. colonized, privileged vs. disadvantaged) and therefore has its own particular forms of governance, techniques, economies, politics, and geographies (see, for instance, Foucault, 2007). One of the fundamental strategies of the hegemony-seeking power that is in operation across the Asia-Pacific region is the exclusion of peoples from the realm of the "citizen" of the colonizing power. The inhabitants of the region are treated by faraway governments and militaries as "others" that do not get incorporated into the dominant group's conceptualization of "us." The scholarship of Giorgio Agamben (1998, 2005) is useful for understanding this colonial situation. In his work Agamben points out that there is a big difference in the way governments and other powerful entities treat people who are merely physically alive and people who are considered part of the body politic (people who, in a sense, have a politically recognized and valued life). The people in this recognized "in-group" have rights to political representation, are subject to legal protections, and are granted access to state programs for the maintenance of their health, productivity, and security.[2] People deemed to be outside the "in-group" (people not in the "nation") are not subject to these privileges. Agamben refers to these excluded people as "bare life": people who are biologically alive but do not have lives that a state sees as worthy of political concern or protection. These "bare lives" are seen at worst as potential threats to the lives of "real citizens," and at best as irrelevant.

Given the U.S. military adventurism over the past decade in places such as Iraq, Afghanistan, the Horn of Africa, and the southern Philippines (and the use of locations with dubious political statuses, like Guantánamo, for human rights abuses), there are obvious reasons why this theoretical perspective has become popular in contemporary social science research. In this era of the "War on Terror" and the Obama administration's targeted drone assassinations, Agamben's theories on the marginalization of people and places to the level of disposability has attracted a lot of attention from scholars concerned with geopolitics, warfare, and colonialism (Aguon, 2005, 2006; Coleman & Grove, 2009; Fluri, 2012; Gregory, 2004; Gregory & Pred, 2007; Hannah, 2006; Mbembé, 2003; Minca, 2006, 2007; Sylvester, 2006). This perspective is particularly useful for understanding how colonialism and militarism have unfolded, and how they continue to operate, in the Pacific region. Thomas Lemke (2005), expounding on Agamben, notes that in Western political history, "the main line of separation is not the difference between friend and enemy, but the distinction between bare life (zoé) and political existence (bíos), between the natural existence and the legal status of a human being" (p. 5). In the context of European and American history this distinction is usually based on racism (Foucault, 2003), but discrimination based on gender, class, political affiliation, and sexuality often come into play as well (Fluri, 2012; Sylvester, 2006).

Looking through this lens we see a political basis for American militarization and colonization in the Pacific region as well as a tolerance by the U.S. state for its deleterious effects. To the U.S. state, the lives of people on colonized islands can be jeopardized or sacrificed not because the people there are enemies but because, politically, they are not even recognized as fully human. They are viewed instead as bare life—as breathing meat, but little else. As Henry Kissinger famously said about American-controlled Micronesia in the wake of nuclear weapons testing, "There are only 90,000 people out there. Who gives a damn?" (G. Johnson, 1980).

These practices of exclusion and domination are the common threads that unite the processes of militarization and colonialism. Both of these processes (as well as other processes of domination, such as patriarchy and racism) can be thought of as *sovereignty-violating machines*. I employ this term to evoke similarities to what Michael Hardt and Antonio Negri (2000) refer to as "sovereignty machines" while pointing out some crucial differences. Discussing the concept of sovereignty, Hardt and Negri (2000) point out that many early European political theorists, such as Hobbes and Rousseau, see the foundation of modern sovereign governance as stemming from the alienation of individuals' rights to the larger community (and into the person of "the sovereign") in exchange for the order and protection that inclusion in the community affords (p. 85). Under situations of colonialism or military domination, however, the process of constructing sovereignty is a purely negative process. The new regime of colonial or militarized sovereignty is not chosen but imposed. It violates the existing individual and collective sovereignties, and then—far from including these people and their political will in the new "community"—it purposefully excludes them. The new subjects created by these sovereignty-violating machines are not part of the wider community that rules them, but are instead dominated "bare lives" denied political representation, social inclusion, and legal protections.

This connects to another of Agamben's (1998) concepts; that of *Homo sacer*, or the "sacrificial person." These are persons excluded from the body politic and left outside its legal protections. A *Homo sacer* can be killed (or tortured, or "let die"), but the act does not legally count as murder because the individual is not considered by the state to be a person in the political sense. *Homo sacer* is a marker of subhumanity applied to those that may threaten the state or the "in-group." This figure has been given various labels throughout history: the terrorist, the enemy combatant, the colonized, the savage, the slave, the contagious. While many theorists use Nazism and concentration camps as an extreme example of this kind of politics, Achille Mbembé (2003) points out that it was through colonialism that many of these horrific practices of governance and justification for state violence came into being. As is clear from reading the accounts of contact and colonialism in the Pacific, the people in the island Pacific have never been included by European, Japanese, or American governments as fully human in the political sense or as in the "in-group" (Dening, 1996; Hezel, 1995; Howe, 2000; Rogers, 1994; B. Smith, 1992; Wilson, 2000). This perspective has marked the inhabitants of the region as "bare life"—as people who can be "helped" by colonial governments, imposed upon by colonial governments, contaminated with radioactivity by colonial governments, fight in the military for a colonial government, but never fully be members of the colonizer's society. The current situation of citizenship on Pacific military islands, as evidenced by U.S. court decisions like the Insular Cases and by "citizenship" agreements such as the Marshall Islands' Compact of Free Association with the U.S. and Guam's Organic Act, demonstrates that the denial of full citizenship continues—a denial caused by the centuries-old confluence of racism, militarism, and colonialism (Herman, 2008). This practice of social inclusion and exclusion that is a fundamental basis of colonialism is also a basis for all politics of hegemony. It divides the social terrain into the camps of the "enemy" and "us," but it also defines a third group: those who simply don't matter. This third group has suffered greatly when hegemony-seeking powers have collided. These are the people whose deaths are referred to as "collateral damage." These are the people who live at the end of the runway with screaming jets overhead. These are the people kicked off their lands for weapons testing and military bases. These are the people who can never go home because they were removed "for the good of mankind" (Niedenthal, 2001).

There is, however, another way of conceptualizing politics—a political approach that refutes the inclusion/exclusion binary and refuses to label anyone as bare life. There are people across the Pacific region (and the world) who have been reimagining politics along much more inclusive and egalitarian lines, and there are geographers and other social theorists whose work aims to destabilize hegemony-seeking power and supplant it with a different vision for international relationships and security (Kirk, 2008; Koopman, 2011; Loyd, Mitchelson, & Burridge, 2012). As Claudio Minca (2007) asks, "Can geography help theorise a politics that does not need to except bare life, a politics able to discard the spatial devices of 'belonging' and 'population'?" (p. 95). If it listens to the voices of those struggling against contemporary militarization and colonialism, I believe that it can.

Affinity-Seeking Power

Most people are familiar with the techniques and consequences of the endless battles for hegemony. What, however, are the political techniques and strategies that follow from the simple ethic that the "other" is something we strive to hold affinity with, not something to be repelled or sacrificed? What happens when we view ourselves, regardless of our differences, as all being "us" (Hardt & Negri, 2004)? What are the techniques, economies, politics, and geographies produced by an ethic of inclusion and affinity? What strategies for "security" are produced? Furthermore, what kinds of places are produced when actions are driven by that ethic? Are they places full of razor wire, border walls, prisons, and military bases? No.

While scholars have paid a lot of attention to processes and strategies for hegemony in the region, far less scholarship and political action has been oriented toward analyzing and enhancing the role of affinity-based approaches to politics (though see important exceptions such as Aguon, 2006; Kirk, 2008; Shigematsu & Camacho, 2010; Wilson, 2000). There is, as noted, a "hegemony of hegemony" (Day, 2005). That is, the idea that hegemony and domination is the only way political power operates, and therefore the only way to wage or analyze political battles, is itself a hegemonic idea. I argue that political actors and researchers would be well served to look behind the hegemony of hegemony and develop an affinity for affinity.

There are many powerful groups in the region using affinity-seeking power, actively and successfully struggling to rid their local places of the military machinery of hegemony-seeking power and working toward a different vision of Pacific politics. These groups can be characterized as "newest social movements," which Richard Day (2005) theorizes as different from what he refers to as "old social movements" and "new social movements." In Day's characterization, "old social movements," such as communist and anticolonial political parties, desire to take over the state apparatus through political or revolutionary means so the party can then wield state power on behalf of an oppressed class, ethnicity, or social group. New social movements, on the other hand, consist of oppressed identity groups who decry their lack of rights compared with dominant social groups and then demand that the state expand those rights. Examples of these kinds of movements would be civil rights movements demanding equality for women or for people from oppressed racial groups or sexual orientations. While these two types of social movements have different approaches to dealing with the state, they both strengthen the position of the state through appeals to its power and authority.

In contrast to both of these strategies, the "newest" social movements treat the state not as a site for the redress of injustices, but as a corrupt organ that is the origin and defender of exploitative and unjust social relations. Like movements characterized as the "New Left" (Breines, 1980; Katsiaficas, 1987), these movements attempt to rectify social, environmental, political, and economic grievances by building alternative institutions to the state and attempting to limit or abolish the state's power in particular spaces. The goal of newest social movements, then, is not to take over the existing state apparatus or to recognize rights for a group within the state system, but to negate the state's ability to define and arbitrate rights. In place of the current hierarchical state, these groups advocate for local governance centered on the politics of affinity rather than hegemony or domination.

Of course, these categorizations of activism into old, new, and newest are just that: categorizations. All three of these political strategies have existed side-by-side throughout history, and while some strategies may have been dominant at different time periods—with tactics of state refusal and displacement currently in ascendency—in practice many contemporary social movements in the Pacific engage in some combination of all three of these approaches. My motivation for applying these theoretical perspectives to my discussion of antimilitary activism in colonized places is not to determine whether the activist groups qualify as a certain type of movement or to test a theory using these groups as a case study. Rather, I wish to weave the theoretical perspectives on recent currents in social movements with descriptions of these groups' activities to show how each can inform the other as well as to better theorize how communities can achieve more egalitarian, demilitarized, and peaceful futures.

As far as tactics, the affinity-seeking power of the newest social movements operates differently from hegemony-seeking forms of activism. As Day (2005) suggests, traditional forms of social movements have been oriented toward taking over the machinery of domination so that their will (allegedly a more "just" one) can then dominate. This orientation leads to organizing tactics whereby groups seeking to impose hegemony exploit the energy of movements to build political machines (parties) or to bend the will of other individuals and groups toward favored agendas. This political strategy merely attempts to exchange one form of domination for another and to switch the class of individuals that command the heights of a hierarchy. On a national scale this approach can be exemplified by countries going from capitalist domination to a Leninist-style "dictatorship of the proletariat," or from an exploitative colonial government run by corrupt colonial officials to an exploitative postcolonial government run by corrupt indigenous officials. On a more local scale it might be enacted as a political candidate or party showing up at a protest merely to gain adherents and promote an agenda. Practitioners of affinity politics would hold that this quest for hegemony does not overcome relationships of domination—it just reproduces them.

Solidarity based on affinity is different. It is solidarity without attempt to channel or "organize" others. It is a desire "for non-universalizing, non-hierarchical, non-coercive relationships based on mutual aid and shared ethical commitments" (Day, 2005, p. 9). It comes from a space of recognizing that nobody is more or less qualified, more or less pure, more or less able to speak, than others. Affinity politics is based on holding solidarity with others, regardless of differences, for the purpose of undoing relationships of domination not just "out there" but between activists as well. It is not just an outcome or goal, but rather a commitment to a process. This approach is strong within antimilitarization activist groups at local levels and also repeats from island to island. While the movements are not devoid of attempts at hegemony-based organizing, there are strong commitments to consensus decision making, local autonomy, solidarity, and being watchful of relationships of domination within and between activist circles.

These approaches are nurtured and supported within these newest social movements not just because they are niceties that garnish the main thrust of antimilitarization activism (getting the military off the islands), but because they are absolutely intrinsic to the larger project of redefining security away from militarized notions toward person-centered views of "genuine security." This kind of security comes not only from limiting the power of the state through protests or the removal of militarization, but from a vision of and ability to produce the cultural, economic, and political processes and institutions that can maintain genuine security in place. These methods of organizing and communicating in activist circles are not just tactics for winning a political battle, but the foundations of different forms of being that actively supplant those of the state-centered society. While the slow work of building these networks of affinity may not be as noticeable or flashy as people cutting fences and getting dragged away by police, they are every bit as indispensable for creating a world where security comes from affinity and connection rather than domination and military violence.

The Geographies of Hegemony

This form of activism and political mobilization has the potential to destabilize the traditional geographies of geopolitics. Hegemony-seeking power has a particular geography: a particular way it arrays itself across space and a way it produces the places and spaces it requires. It is a geography of binaries: of dominators and dominated, colonizer and colonized, citizens and "bare life," centers and peripheries. Borders and borderlands are, in this sense, an effect of that hegemony-seeking power. It is a constructed periphery of power and the leading edge where it is deployed (Morehouse, 2004; R. Jones, 2012; Loyd et al., 2012). The geographies of hegemony-seeking power are traditionally conceptualized in terms of a nested hierarchy of spatially contiguous spaces. Doreen Massey (2004) characterized this hierarchy as the "Russian Doll" model of looking at power and scale, where each scale includes inside it the finer, more local scales. In this model, the globe is divided into countries, which are divided into states or provinces, which are divided into cities and towns, which are divided into neighborhoods, and so on. More recently, however, there has been more interest in describing power as flowing not evenly across contiguous spaces, but rather through networks that may span different spatial extents of the world, that are more connected and concentrated in some places or "nodes" while weak or absent in others (Appadurai, 1996; Campbell, 1996; Castells, 1996; Massey, 1991; Thrift, 1995). Much of the discussion of networks of power pertains to the economic and cultural manifestations of globalization, but it is equally applicable to political geographies (Herod & Wright, 2002).

As Agnew (2009) points out, however, power is never simply territorial *or* networked.[3] He argues for a view of power that incorporates *both* aspects. While territory-based entities, like nation-states, aim to be able to surveil and project power over the totality of the spaces they are nominally in control of, in practice this aim is usually not fully realized. A state's ability to control space is always incomplete, spatially variable, and therefore in a way "networked." Even though spaces may be within the boundaries of a country such as the United States, the state may have great difficulty surveilling and controlling some places like the canyon lands of northern Arizona, remote valleys on Moloka'i, or my kitchen. Also, a state does have the ability to project power in a networked fashion far outside its territory (this is especially true of the United States), but again it is spatially variable. For example, the American state may be able to easily project power to Okinawa, Kabul, or Guam but have great difficulty surveilling and securing rural areas of Afghanistan and Somalia. Hegemony-seeking power may be able to be projected great distances—even well beyond the borders of a nation-state—but that is not to say that power can be projected *everywhere*. The project of hegemony-seeking power then becomes to increasingly widen its network and incorporate more and more of the "blank spots" that are outside its network of power (regardless of whether they are within the official geographic borders) in order to maintain its dominance and to counter resistance that may be arising from these spaces (Scott, 2009).

Another important aspect of viewing power as being both networked and territorial is that there are many other agents besides states that have the ability to manage activities within nations and also to manage global networks and flows. Agnew (2009) cites numerous examples of these: transnational corporations, drug cartels, organized religions, pirates, financial institutions and traders, Al Qaeda, and the International Monetary Fund. What these actors and institutions have in common is that they are all able to project power through networks without any large contiguous territorial base. This is not to say these actors are "nonterritorial." They do have to exist *somewhere*. They tend, however, to control noncontiguous archipelagos of space (camps, headquarter buildings, etc.) enmeshed within the spaces of (possibly multiple) sovereign states. To tease out this interplay between territorial sovereignty and networks of power, Agnew (2009) introduces the useful idea of *effective sovereignty* that views power in this way:

> Sovereignty is made out of the circulation of power among a range of actors at dispersed sites rather than simply emanating outward from an original and commanding central point such as an abstracted "state." Michel Foucault captures something of this approach when he writes, "The state is nothing more than the mobile effect of a regime of multiple governmentalities," meaning that any given

> state is a centralized deposit of sovereign (police, military), disciplinary (including surveillance and punishment) and bio-political (medico-corporeal, citizenship, entitlements) powers that while historically concentrated in governmental institutions are *often exercised by and can be captured by other actors.* (p. 9, emphasis added)

So according to this formulation, power is not solely the realm of officially recognized states with territories. Of course if we look again at the list of other actors capable of practicing effective sovereignty without seizing a state and territory, we see a long list of villains that are still engaged in hegemony-seeking power. Not many would say the world is better off being run by the likes of transnational corporations, drug cartels, organized religions, pirates, financial institutions and traders, Al Qaeda, and the International Monetary Fund. In some respects we could add the U.S. military to this list. Even though it is clearly associated with and directed by the American state, it is an arm that manages flows and processes clearly outside the borders of U.S. territory. In other words, its effective sovereignty, like that of the other entities on the list, regularly impinges on the territorial sovereignty of other nation-states.

Many people are concerned with the motives, morality, and accountability of these extraterritorial actors (Agnew, 2009). These agents, many of which can be characterized as agents of "globalization," are not subject to the same political pressures as states. Since they are divorced from territory—and since citizenship and voting rights are associated with territory—their accountability to democratic processes can be questioned. Cypriots do not get to vote for the head of the IMF making decisions about their economy. People in northern Mexico do not get to vote on which cartel is going to control local politics. When Okinawans vote to close or block the new construction of U.S. military bases, the U.S. military does not have to heed the results. As state power has decreased under campaigns of neoliberalization, some progressive political activists have voiced concern about where the power is going as it is subtracted from the state. Concern over this expansion of the effective sovereignty of nonstate actors is exemplified by Noam Chomsky's (1998) position that when you minimize the state you do not eliminate decision making, decisions just get made somewhere else—namely, by corporations and other entities seeking hegemony and domination.

The Geographies of Affinity

While the list of nonstate agents practicing effective sovereignty shown above does not offer much hope for a better future beyond the state, I argue that affinity-seeking organizations can also use the concept of effective sovereignty and its associated noncontiguous spatiality for egalitarian aims. After all, there are obvious connections between the idea of effective sovereignty and Richard Day's "newest social movements" that aim to supplant the power of the state with a power based on consensus and affinity. When decision-making power is transferred from the state to another organization, the qualities of that organization determine what those decisions will look like. Establishing spaces of effective sovereignty need not be the purview only of states, terrorist groups, and bankers. It can also be a strategy employed by groups and individuals seeking a demilitarized and decolonized future.

As affinity-seeking power differs from hegemony-seeking power, its spatialities differ as well. While also seeking to expand spatially, affinity-seeking power is deployed to level hierarchies instead of maintaining or re-creating them. It therefore has some differences in how it deploys across space and produces places and spaces. In other words, it has a different imagined geography. Traditionally, affinity-seeking power could also be looked at as operating in nested "Russian doll" scales. Relationships of affinity and mutual aid have long been associated with the local (Karatani, 2008). People who are tied to each other through kinship and common residence have often looked to others in their locality as having an affinity (with the obvious glaring exception of close-by stigmatized "others" that are found in almost every space and time period). The lineage, the tribe, the village, the neighborhood, the city, the nation: communities whose members imagine themselves to have commonalities have often been associated with some kind of spatially contiguous grouping (Anderson, 1991). Some have praised the local for these traits and argue that moving the locus of politics to that scale, away from the more abstracting and hierarchical national and global scales, can result in a more egalitarian existence (Bookchin, 1982; Hayes-Conroy, 2008). However, some criticize the insularity, exclusiveness, and xenophobia that can exist in the local and express concerns that relying on a spatially closed local network of affinity can lead to reactionary politics and even fascism (Harvey, 1996).

Words like *community* and concepts like "buy local" urge people to operate from a position of affinity with neighbors, but is there room for expanding this sphere of the "nation" and projecting affinity across space? As Kojin Karatani (2008) points out, such expansion is not only possible but has been happening for quite some time. Projects that aim to create communities of affinity across space have been common throughout history. Religions (most notably Christianity, Judaism, Islam, and Buddhism) are the most obvious example of an attempt to transcend localism and bring people from across widespread areas into relationships of affinity (Walker, 1993). Marxist internationalism, anarchist conceptualizations of international mutual aid, and the development of a "transnational bourgeoisie" would be other examples (Agnew, 1993; Kropotkin, 1885). More recently, Karatani's (2008) work on "associationism"—along with others who see the rise of a "coming community" (Agamben, 1993) or a "swarm" of the "global multitude" (Hardt & Negri, 2000, 2004)—also theorizes that a contemporary spatially fluid global movement of solidarity can rise against the exclusionary and exploitative triad of capital/nation/state.[4]

While specifically revolutionary or anticapitalist efforts to stretch solidarity over global scales may not be as prominent as some of these scholars hope they may one day be, it is fairly clear that the technological innovations of the past century have stretched other relationships of affinity. People in the many parts of the world have friends or relatives who are from, or may have migrated to, places across the globe and therefore may have personal connections that lead them to care about political issues and oppression even when it is happening in a country where they have never been. Likewise, some countries, particularly in the island Pacific, have so many of their citizens living in other countries that the "nation" is defined more by belonging to a kinship or cultural network than living in a locality (Lilomaiava-Doktor, 2009). While these networks may not be radical in and of themselves, they lay the groundwork for an expanded "geography of responsibility" by developing an ethic of caring for people at a distance (Massey, 2004; Robinson, 1999). As geographers over the past century and a half from Peter Kropotkin (1885) to Doreen Massey (2004) have pointed out, it is an important political project to expand these geographies of responsibility and affinity to increase the number of people we consider to be "us" rather than "them."

Turning these expanded networks of care into social movements, however, has been more difficult. Projects for expanding realms of solidarity have been unsuccessful for reasons too numerous to give an exhaustive listing. Attempts at internationalism have been derailed by national rivalries, national projects by class rivalries, class consciousness by racism, antiracism solidarity by gender discrimination, and so on. While some of the reasons for these failures have been differences of opinion about which axis of identity (class, race, ethnicity, language, gender, sexuality, etc.) is the most salient one, in a larger sense it is hegemony-seeking power that has routinely derailed these affinity-seeking projects. Within activist spaces there is a tendency toward contests over making certain groups, or at least certain ideas, hegemonic. Many activists and researchers have pointed out that activist networks, even those espousing nonhierarchical, affinity-based tactics of organizing, are still networks with internal conflicts and uneven distributions of power. As theorists of social movements have shown, individuals and groups come to a network with unequal access to resources and different levels of privilege, so an organization cannot be devoid of differences in power (Cumbers, Routledge, & Nativel, 2008; Day, 2005; Koopman, 2011). Some groups and individuals, often academics or professionals based in the wealthier countries, function as "supernodes" in the activist networks because of their ability to marshal resources and do the extensive travel to global meetings, like World Social Forums and the global antimilitary base meeting detailed in chapter 6 (Cumbers et al., 2008, p. 190).

The fact that these "newest" social movements claim to be egalitarian in their aims but are still lumpy with power differences does not mean they should be discounted as hypocritical, impure, or ineffective. It is not surprising that groups seeking affinity and the leveling of hierarchies have some of the same struggles within them as exist in the larger society. After all, they are constructed out of existing social relations, even if they are trying to transcend them. As John Holloway (2002) puts it, activists "cannot start by pretending to stand outside the dissonance of our own experience for to do so would be a lie" (p. 5). He adds that social criticism does not "come riding up on a white horse with the hope of kissing the world into life: it is the life of the world" (p. 98). In other words, activists are not above the problems they are seeking to transcend. For instance, I characterize the antimilitarization groups I focus on in this book as being both *of* and *against* the empire. They are embedded in a problematic and hegemony-filled social environment yet strive to build bridges of solidarity to reshape it. From this perspective there is no oppressed "other" that the activist is either saving or fighting against. Instead, there is just an expanding "us" (S. Davis, 2012). These groups, despite having to deal with the inherent paradoxes of being and acting in an uneven terrain of power, still offer an alternative to politics based on the pursuit of hegemony. By seeking affinity, these movements and networks operate differently, both internally and externally, and are important contemporary nonstate actors in international affairs.

These groups' searches for affinity across borders are reformulating the spaces where effective politics can occur and redefining the spatiality of ethics and care. Geographically these networks of affinity look very similar to the other nonstate actors practicing effective sovereignty mentioned above. They are archipelagos of individuals and spaces constructing a networked imagined community. These networks are stretched across territorial boundaries and peppered throughout the internal space of existing nation-states. The potential in this spatial form of organizing is enormous. There are many nonstate actors who have immense power through effective sovereignty, but have no explicit territorial sovereignty in the traditional Westphalian system of countries. Developing and deploying this effective sovereignty across space is a potential new spatiality of resistance to destructive state practices such as colonialism and militarism. In other words, you don't have to pursue territorial sovereignty to practice effective sovereignty. Pursuing a networked effective sovereignty is a strategy that could have great benefits for people and groups who have struggled in their attempts to gain territorial sovereignty or for whom traditional territorial approaches to sovereignty make little sense: transnational movements, communities without states, migrating communities, diaspora communities, and those in places still under colonialism (such as the islands examined in this book). It is also useful for both political analysis and activist tactics in sea spaces, traditionally viewed as outside the realm of territorial sovereignty (Steinberg, 2001). Current political hot spots such as the Senkaku/Diaoyu Islands in the East China Sea and the Spratly Islands in the South China Sea are prime examples. They are the sites of disputes over territorial sovereignty, and they are critical paths in the networks of world trade. They are also the sites of innovative political proposals (such as the idea that the islands should be shared) that aim to undermine the concept of mutually exclusive territorial sovereignty ("Intellectuals," 2013).

By seeking common ground in ever-growing networks and by challenging traditional nationalistic geographies of territorial sovereignty and rivalry, these movements bring forward the question of how far these boundaries of solidarity should extend. Following on the work of poststructuralist feminists, Day (2005) promotes the radical position that the boundaries of solidarity need to be pushed in more than just a territorially expansive sense. Instead, the whole idea of affinity-*seeking* power is just that: it is a project that *continually seeks* affinity. Day refers to these social movements as operating according to the principle of "groundless solidarity driven by infinite responsibility" (p. 179). By "groundless solidarity" he is referring to the idea that people hold solidarity with each other because all oppressions (and privileges) are linked and therefore no one axis of oppression (race, class, gender, ability, sexuality, etc.) is privileged. "Infinite responsibility" suggests that there is no edge, spatial or social, at which we stop having responsibility to keep *seeking* affinity. It means "always being open to the challenge of another Other, always being ready to hear a voice that points out how one is not adequately in solidarity, despite one's best efforts" (Day, 2005, p. 18). Geographers promoting an "open sense of place" also encourage this method for social activism. Larsen and Johnson (2012) state, "An open sense of place is anarchic: Its praxis discourages totalizing theoretical statements in favor of a commitment to *not knowing* that catalyzes spontaneous interactions with others in an attitude of openness and receptivity" (p. 643, emphasis added). In other words, affinity-seeking power, like hegemony-seeking power, is a continual *process* that constantly challenges limits, including personal ones, and looks to new geographic and social territories. Advocates for peace and justice can follow the advice of pan-Asian scholar Sun Ge (2003), who contends that "to establish a truly egalitarian perspective, we must discard a narrow nationalist mode of thinking and avoid its dependence on existing political and social foundations" (p. 43).

Although I contain most of my discussion in this book to antimilitarization social movements in the Asia-Pacific region, I think the radical possibilities of affinity-seeking politics go beyond the region and also go beyond a demilitarized future. They also go beyond merely different, more horizontal, structures for organizing activist networks. Though affinity-seeking power does tend to travel with a flatter, more consensus-based organizational style, it is more than that. Affinity seeking is more a guiding universal ethic than an organizational model or activist tactic. As I hope is evident through the stories I tell in this book, it is an ethic with deep roots in the Pacific region and one that continues to grow in the edge between empires.[5]

The Structure of the Book

Despite a strong temptation to arrange this book geographically and look at each site of militarization separately, I have chosen to examine the subject thematically. While this approach sometimes requires breaking up the stories of what is happening on the individual islands, I think that the fluid nature of American imperialism—and the way the military base network has shifted from place to place—necessitates a broad view of the contexts in which these islands experience militarization. I can tell the story I am trying to tell more effectively by foregrounding the *processes* of hegemony- and affinity-seeking political action and then grounding the analysis of those processes in the places I examine.

Most of the narrative in this book is analytical in nature, but interspersed throughout are more descriptive ruminations based on observations of the island landscapes being discussed. My intention is that the descriptive sections will add some flesh to the bones of the analytical writing as well as give readers a better feel for the landscapes I am writing about. There is always a danger when anyone is representing and writing about landscapes, especially ones that have been the sites of such extensive imperial intervention, that the representations will be incomplete and biased (Duncan & Ley, 1993; M. L. Pratt, 1992). Since any representation of a place is from an imbedded, situated perspective, this possibility is unavoidable. However, I attempt to present these experiences of place not as authoritative accounts of what the places are "really like" but as my impressions that are, like anyone's, based on partial and embodied experiences. By writing about these examples of the American military presence in the region, and by showing photographs from these sites, I aim to help the reader better understand the on-the-ground consequences of imperial control.

I then link these descriptive sections with information from informants as well as an analysis of broader-scale processes in an attempt to "connect the dots" and weave together the story of politics in the region.

In chapter 2 I begin by introducing the "Baseworld" through an analysis of the network of military bases and a description of their sites, using the example of Kwajalein Atoll in the Marshall Islands. I look at where the bases are, but, more importantly, I look at why the bases are located where they are. I argue that there have been profound shifts in the rationale for base placement in response to a variety of factors. While some shifts have resulted from particular crises and wars, major changes in the structure of the global military presence have also resulted from changes in military doctrine and technologies. The current assemblage of bases is an important departure from previous strategies of base alignment. My goal is to give readers not only the global view of American power but also my grounded view of visiting and researching the sites of U.S. bases. Using the perspectives of critical feminist geopolitics to guide my discussion, I then go on to show how these global imperatives and grounded experiences entwine to affect each other in these geopolitically critical places.

In chapter 3 I present a detailed discussion of the American use of Bikini Atoll in the Marshall Islands, a radioactive nuclear test site long abandoned by the United States. The atoll no longer has any active role in the functioning of the U.S. military, but it provides an excellent case study of how the U.S. military "sees" places, how it reconstructs inhabited places for its own purposes, and what the consequences are for the people who live there. The Americans took possession of Bikini at the end of World War II for nuclear weapons testing, and the site's transformation therefore took place at a critical juncture in American history (the beginning of the U.S. role as a world power) and for a particularly important purpose (demonstrating the power of nuclear weapons to the rest of the world when only the United States possessed them). Simply put, the first presentation of American hegemony to the world was performed on the stage of Bikini Atoll. Of course, the fact that Bikini Atoll was an inhabited homeland in 1946 was a problem for the U.S. military. The techniques used to permanently remove the inhabitants against their wishes were to become a blueprint for similar acts of dispossession across the Pacific. I discuss Bikini Atoll in chapter 3 because it introduces this imperial "way of seeing" and geographic myth creation that is still repeated to this day.

In the following chapters I go into detail about environmental and social problems at sites of U.S. military bases and the resistance movements that arise in these places. In chapter 4 I give an account of militarization and in-place resistance in Hawai'i, Okinawa, and Vieques (Puerto Rico) as well as the ways in which the military has responded to those resistances. Vieques is obviously not in the Pacific region, but the story of what happened there is critical for understanding how resistance movements in the Pacific operate. Vieques is probably best known in activist circles for accomplishing something amazing: it is a small colonial island that managed to organize and kick out the U.S. military. Due to grassroots organizing and an orchestrated civil disobedience campaign, the U.S. military was forced to leave Vieques in 2003. Solidarity networks between people in militarized islands in Latin America and the Pacific region are quite strong, and the networks have shared tactics and provided mutual support.

In the latter part of chapter 4 I also examine how the U.S. military has reacted to these effective in-place resistances by shifting the network of bases to sites with greater colonial domination, such as Guam and the Northern Mariana Islands. While antimilitarization advocates in some countries have had some successes, often these successes merely shift where the military goes. Such shifts have certainly affected Guam. Guam has been a U.S. possession since 1898. The island was taken by Japan at the beginning of World War II but was then reoccupied by the Americans near the end of the war after a bloody battle with the Japanese military. Since that time it has been an important site in the U.S. military network. Citizens in Guam do not have voting representation in the United States, and the United Nations currently lists Guam as a colony. As a result, the citizens of Guam cannot easily affect U.S. military policy, but military policy certainly affects them. Close to one-third of the island's land is in the hands of the military, much of it simply taken from original landowners with little or no compensation. Furthermore, the military has described the coming Guam military expansion as the largest military restructuring project by the United States since the end of World War II. Estimates suggest that in the coming years, close to 50,000 residents will be *added* to the current population of approximately 160,000 due to the impending buildup of U.S. forces there (S. Davis, 2011).

In chapter 5 I examine how militarization and colonization interact with local island environments. While it is fairly well documented that military activities, especially training and weapons testing, contaminate local environments, it is less appreciated how complex some of the interactions between colonialism, militarization, and the environment can be. I introduce the concept of the "colonial/military/tourism/environment nexus" to describe the interacting and reinforcing ways in which these processes can not only harm environments but also perpetuate social injustice. Using examples from Guam and the Marshall Islands, I explore the paradox of how labels like *pristine* and *natural* are applied to militarized landscapes to deepen colonial relations, restrict civilian access to contaminated areas, and justify the continued militarization of occupied lands.

In chapter 6 I examine how local social movements have responded to the continued colonization and militarization of the region. I first document how activists are deploying affinity-seeking power in global networks to contest the island-to-island regional maneuvering by the military. By focusing my discussion on the international "No Bases" movement and their global conference in Ecuador in 2007, I detail some of the debates within the movement and also discuss some of the promises and challenges activists face when they try to take local resistance movements and rescale them at the global level. In the latter half of the chapter I conclude with a discussion that ties together some of the themes brought up over the course of the book and an examination of the ramifications and potential new directions for politics in the Asia-Pacific region. I also try to situate Pacific activism in the global realm of geopolitics and ask questions about its significance. Can affinity-seeking power stand strong and have a real impact on systems of hegemony-seeking power, or must it hide in the margins, relegated to subtle techniques of subversion? Can systems of affinity-seeking power tear down existing hierarchies without developing others? I argue that both are possible and that the small, colonized islands of the Pacific have a story to share. It is a story that can facilitate the efforts of researchers, activists, and residents working to redefine security and transcend the trap of pursuing hegemony.

CHAPTER 2

Surveying the Baseworld

Maintaining global hegemony is both an expansive and an expensive project. To project power globally, the United States has relied on a network of bases, training areas, and weapons-testing facilities scattered around the world. While having the world's largest navy and employing such technological innovations as longer-range transports, bombers, and drones have extended the spatial reach of the U.S. military, the United States is still dependent on a collection of land bases around the globe. Referred to by some as the "Baseworld" (C. Johnson, 2004), this collection of U.S. military bases (and their associated training areas and support facilities) can be viewed at one scale as nodes in a global network, but they can also be viewed as individual sites with complex histories and geographies of lived experience (Enloe, 2000; Gillem, 2007; Grossman, 2002; Lutz, 2009). To frame military operations at the regional scale on the Pacific edge of the American Empire, it is useful to examine both U.S. global basing strategies and individual militarized sites. In this chapter I do both. I start with a close look at the base at Kwajalein Atoll in the Marshall Islands and then broaden the discussion through an examination of the contemporary U.S. basing strategy.

The base at Kwajalein is a center for the development of a weapon system that is central to U.S. military strategy in Asia and other parts of the world: missile defense. While ballistic missile defense systems (or "Star Wars," as they have been called) are ostensibly defensive, they also figure into offensive military strategies, as well as strategies aimed at protecting the trade system in the western Pacific, by limiting the ability of potential adversaries (China and North Korea) to deploy missiles as deterrents to forward-deployed American military forces. In other words, these systems do not just ward off enemy attacks; they also make it potentially less costly for the United States to attack others, since adversaries will be less able to retaliate. These systems give the U.S. military a freer hand in the region and the U.S. government additional military leverage. I hope my discussion of Kwajalein Atoll shows that missile defense systems not only heighten the likelihood of U.S.-led military conflicts in Asia but also have some serious consequences for the people unfortunate enough to host their development, testing, and deployment.

Military Colonialism and American Perceptions

In an early morning lecture at the University of Vermont I once asked the students, "How many of you have heard of missile defense testing?" Almost all arms in the class went up. So I asked, "OK, what is missile defense testing?" A student near the front offered, "It's the military program where they are trying to figure out how to shoot down incoming missiles." Another student chimed in, "Even though they keep spending a lot of money on it, it hasn't really worked, right?"

"Well, there is some debate on what you mean by 'worked,'" I answered, "but yes, it is an expensive program. Does anyone know where it takes place?"

In a room of 150 American college geography students, not a single hand went up.

"Has anyone ever heard of Kwajalein Atoll in the Marshall Islands?" Again, no hands went up. This did not necessarily surprise me. In the case of Kwajalein, most Americans do not question what occurs there because, quite simply, they have never heard of the place. When media reports discuss missile defense testing, they rarely mention Kwajalein Atoll. Instead, they say that the tests occur in that indistinct space usually referred to as "over the Pacific."

Kwajalein Atoll, however, is a real place, and the American weapons testing that occurs there has real consequences to the thousands of people that call it home (see maps 1 and 2 in chapter 1 and map 3 in this chapter). The atoll is a collection of nearly one hundred connected islands that stretch in a loop for over one hundred miles around an enclosed lagoon. It is the largest coral atoll in the world. While some people may assume that islands in the Pacific are largely uninhabited, this is usually not the case. Kwajalein Atoll, for instance, has close to twenty thousand inhabitants. The atoll was settled by Micronesian navigators over two thousand years ago, but it is best known historically for being the site of a major battle between the Japanese and Americans in World War II. After this battle, the United States turned the largest southernmost island into a military base, and it remains one to this day. This island is referred to as Kwajalein Island, the same name as the whole atoll.

The use of the atoll as a testing range predates the "Star Wars" missile defense testing program. Since the 1960s the atoll has been used as the target for testing ballistic missiles. Missiles designed to be part of the U.S. nuclear arsenal are launched from California to see how accurately they can strike targets on Kwajalein. The problem with this target practice is that the atoll is inhabited, and launching missiles experimentally toward people is a recipe for disaster. The military solution to this problem was not to test the missiles elsewhere, but rather to force the local Marshallese people off almost all the islands of the atoll and restrict most of the population to the small island of Ebeye. The vast

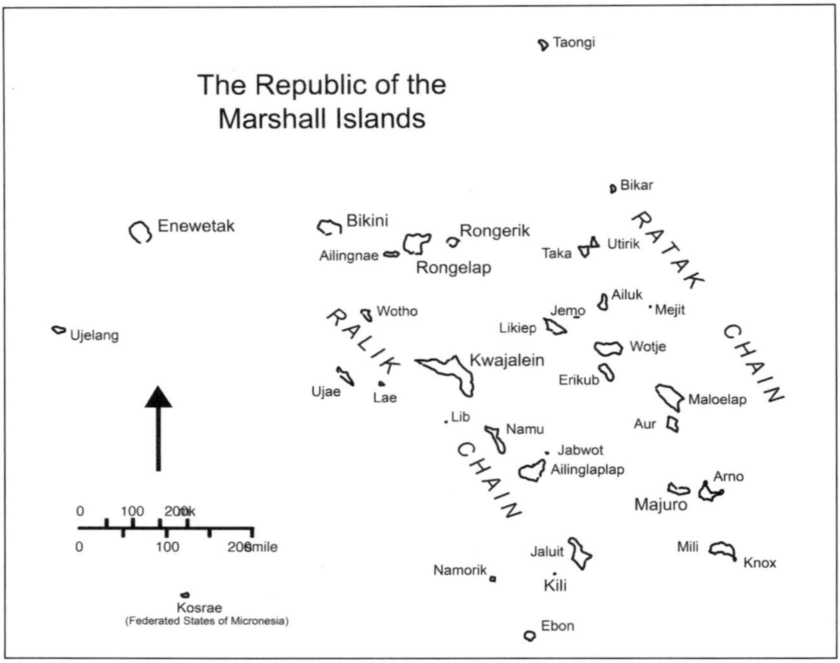

MAP 3. The Marshall Islands. Map by author.

majority of the atoll became the "mid-atoll corridor," an area swept of habitation and off-limits to fishing or other uses by the native population of the islands. Kwajalein Island, the biggest island of the atoll and the traditional center of Marshallese life, was turned into the operational base for missile testing and became an enclave of U.S. military personnel and technicians. The island was rendered off-limits to Marshallese except to work as low-wage laborers who must get off the island after their shifts. When, in the 1980s, Ronald Reagan announced the development of the "Strategic Defense Initiative" program, whose aim was to develop a system capable of shooting down enemy ballistic missiles, Kwajalein Atoll became the main site for this testing, and it continues to host this project today.

While Kwajalein is officially part of the Republic of the Marshall Islands, which is technically independent from the United States, the truth on the ground is hard to hide. After gaining their "independence" in the 1980s following four decades of direct colonial rule by the United States (which had followed periods of colonial control by the Japanese, Germans, and Spanish), the Marshall Islands signed a "Compact of Free Association" with the United

States. The Republic of the Marshall Islands (RMI) has some features of independence: an embassy, UN recognition, and some control over domestic affairs. It remains, however, linked to the United States in many ways. RMI citizens can visit and work in the United States without a visa and join the U.S. armed forces. The RMI government gets almost half of its governmental operating budget from the United States (with many strings attached). The RMI also promises the United States "strategic denial," which means that the U.S. military is the only one allowed to use the territory and surrounding waters. At independence the RMI was also granted some annual income for the use of Kwajalein as well as some (woefully inadequate) funds to compensate the country for the legacy of nuclear weapons testing on its formerly populated northern atolls (see chapter 3). So what does the technically independent Kwajalein Atoll, Republic of the Marshall Islands, look like?

Walking through Kwajalein and Ebeye

At the airport on Kwajalein Atoll is a large, conspicuous mural of the atoll commemorating the bloody battle fought on the island between competing foreign powers. The caption celebrates the U.S. victory, noting that the atoll was "Taken from the Japanese: 31 January–5 February 1944."

There is a sharp racial distinction in the experiences of those who have just arrived. White passengers, presumably working on base, exit quickly. The darker-skinned Marshallese sit and wait until a bus with bars on the windows comes to ferry them to the dock, where they are put on a boat to take them to nearby Ebeye. I was processed, photographed, given a badge, and allowed to join the other white passengers. Moving past the mural—*taken from the Japanese*—I walked out into the glaring sunlight of midday Kwajalein.

Getting onto the base on Kwajalein is hard unless you know someone. I did not really know anyone on Kwajalein, but I was living on Majuro Atoll, a few hundred miles to the south, and a friend put me in contact with one of her friends who works on the base. Now that I had a sponsor on base, the difficult became possible.

In the past this base was so secretive that when passengers on the "island-hopper" flight were flying near Kwajalein, they were told to lower their window shades and not look outside. This is no longer the case. I was able to stroll around the base taking pictures of mammoth radars and other installations while people waved at me and asked me if I needed any help finding anything. They told me stories of the various buildings, including a huge one referred to as "Mount Olympus" or "the million-dollar mistake." This huge structure on the west end of the island was supposed to be able to withstand a direct nuclear strike, but once the Cold War ended with the Soviet Union's collapse, work on the building stopped. It was never completed and ended up not being used for anything. I was shown the island's nine-hole golf course and the pools with large, swimming turtles. People pointed out the island's recycling center, the global positioning system's base station for the mid-Pacific, the open-air movie theater, the grocery store, the cafeteria, the Marshallese craft shop, the modern hospital, the elementary school.

The most prominent thing missing from this military base was the military. On a base of over a thousand residents, there were barely a handful of army personnel. The operations on Kwajalein are largely run by "Kwajalein Range Services," a consortium of Lockheed and Bechtel; formerly it was run by Raytheon. It is these large civilian contractors that give the base its character much more than the military does. On my tour of the island I passed very few cars but throngs of people on bicycles. "It's a very environmentally conscious place," one resident offered. "Unlike where we lived back in California, we don't ever have to drive here. Also, it's safer. I don't have to worry about gangs, or my kids doing drugs. This is a great island to raise a family. I never have to worry where they are. It is a bit isolated, though."

Yes, it is a bit isolated. In many respects it is a grand gated community in the mid-Pacific. I heard jokes that it is a wonderful place for the Federal Witness Relocation Program and that many radar technicians are likely ex-Mafia—an exaggeration, perhaps. The geographic isolation of the island is overcome in many ways, however. First, despite being five thousand miles from California, it is somewhat part of it. It lies on the west side of the international dateline, but because the missiles launched at Kwajalein come from California's Vandenberg Air Force Base, they work on California time and California days (the weekends here occur on Sunday and Monday local time). Also, the phones are on a California area code. Thus, a call from Kwajalein to the U.S. mainland is cheap compared with a steeply priced international call to the rest of the Marshalls a few miles away.

The landscape also looks like something out of suburban southern California but with even more palm trees (figure 1). There is a certain common look to U.S. military bases that is a result of conscious planning on the part of the Department of Defense (Gillem, 2007). Buildings are separated for the purposes of protecting people on the base from potential attack, and there is an effort to have U.S. bases the world over follow a general plan that is easily legible to the people who often shuffle from one base to another. The base on Kwajalein is also maintained to be aesthetically pleasing for the Americans that inhabit it. The grass is cut short in the public spaces, on the golf course, and on the

FIGURE 1. Kwajalein Base. Photo by author.

softball fields that lie next to the tennis courts and skate park. The slick, unbroken blacktop roads curve between bungalows and houses surrounded by white wooden fences draped with American flags. The impression of the landscape is unmistakable: this is part of America. The buildings, the amenities, the landscaping all have a functional purpose, but they also serve as constant visual reminders of who has the hegemonic control of the space. This is true all the way down to the detail of what is on the shelves in the grocery store. The local Surfway grocery store is stocked with foods imported from the United States and sold at heavily subsidized prices. In one respect Kwajalein is not like California: it is much cheaper.

Kwajalein is less an army base than it is Pleasantville, USA, for a cadre of scientific technicians and their families. Children raised here, known as "Kwaj kids," often return. I spoke with several adults working on the island who lived there as children, left to go to college, and then fought tooth and nail to get a job back on the island they call home. While waiting in Honolulu for a flight to the Marshalls I overheard a young woman talking to a Christian missionary. The woman explained, "I just graduated from college and I got a job back on Kwaj, where I grew up, thank god. My friends in college gave me crap, saying things like, 'Why would you work for Raytheon? They make evil weapons and bombs and stuff.' I would tell them, 'Yes. But they make evil weapons *on beautiful tropical islands*.'" Such is the attraction of life on Kwaj.

Going from Kwajalein Island to nearby Ebeye is a twenty-minute boat ride into another world. Ebeye is Kwajalein Island's opposite, but not because of its intrinsic nature. Rather, the landscape of Ebeye is the result of its relationship with the nearby base. It is the "host community," a designation it shares with towns across the world from Okinawa to North Carolina. The journey to Ebeye from Kwajalein begins at a small building near the dock. Identity cards are checked and people are herded onto what looks like an amphibious assault landing craft with benches. The boat swings out of the dock and makes good speed over the lagoon water toward Ebeye. The passengers are almost all Marshallese who work at the base. Many of the people are lugging large "jerry cans" of drinkable water from the base to bring to families back on Ebeye. For the twelve-thousand-plus residents of Ebeye there used to be roughly one thousand positions for Marshallese on the base, but the base has slashed that number in recent years. Most of these jobs are low-wage service and nanny jobs that support the American workers on Kwajalein.

Not only must workers return to Ebeye at the end of their shift, the transport of food and other goods from Kwajalein to Ebeye is prohibited. I heard many stories from workers about attempting to bring food, birthday cakes, and other "contraband" items off the base back to Ebeye only to be ordered to throw it away. The reason for this is that the food at the Surfway store on the base is heavily subsidized for the high-paid American workers. Kwajalein officials, as well as shop owners on Ebeye, argue that if Marshallese were allowed to access these subsidized goods and return them to Ebeye, it would undermine the market of high-priced goods available there.

Across from the dock that juts out into the lagoon from Ebeye stand the smashed-together back walls of makeshift houses (figure 2). Half in the water just offshore sits something the size of a bus that is roundish, rusty, and unidentifiable. Due to the use of the rest of the atoll as a site for developing weapons systems, Ebeye lives up to its moniker as "the slum of the Pacific." With well over twelve thousand residents on its one-tenth of a square mile of land, it is one of the most densely populated places on the planet. Health care is rudimentary, and the overcrowded and impoverished conditions are responsible for deadly outbreaks of measles and cholera (French, 2001). Since the Marshallese are blocked from accessing the resources on most of the atoll, and the remaining resources around Ebeye Island are so scant, imported foods are the main source of nourishment. Most of the foods that can survive the long voyage to Ebeye are canned: Spam and corned beef are major staples. The local water

FIGURE 2. Ebeye shoreline. Photo by author.

supply is so unreliable and of such low quality that soda is the preferred drink. Diabetes is rampant, as are the associated amputations caused by the lack of treatment. Not only is the food quality low, the prices for it are so high that the cost of eating in Ebeye makes Honolulu look cheap.

I arrive on Ebeye, throw on my knapsack, and walk to the store a few yards away from the dock. As is common, the island's electricity is not functioning today, and the whir of a portable generator can be heard from the store front. Inside is the antithesis of Kwajalein's Surfway: a sparse selection of packaged breakfast cereal, Spam, soda, and expired potato chips, all at prices remarkably higher than in Kwajalein.

After buying something to drink, I walk around the island. This does not take long. A one-way street runs counterclockwise around the island with a few streets and pathways crisscrossing its width. Most people are indoors avoiding the midday sun, but there are children out and some take an interest in me. A couple of them ask me for money. A few of them ask me for a "high-five" before jokingly withdrawing their hands with speed and fleeing around a corner laughing with glee. A few kids follow me around as I examine the dwellings pressed one against another, the cramped cemeteries on the ocean side of the street, and the crumbling school in the island's center. Other kids pose as I take

FIGURE 3. Ebeye Island looking toward Kwajalein. Photo by author.

photographs of the small clearing where they play with broken plywood "surfboards" in standing puddles of water. They stand like silhouettes in front of the visible massive radars of Kwajalein that point this way and fire high levels of electromagnetic radiation over Ebeye.

The conditions on Ebeye are, by anyone's definition, desperate. What makes the level of desperation truly shocking, however, is that it is caused by one of the most heavily funded American defense projects of the past two decades. The American government gives some money as "rent" to the elite Marshallese landowners of Kwajalein, but it is an embarrassingly low amount compared with the budget of the program as a whole. The rental payments to the Kwajalein landowners are pegged at $15 million a year, while the 2008 missile defense budget was approximately $8.5 billion. (In other words, for every $500 spent on the program, less than $1 is spent compensating the Marshall Islanders.) Furthermore, this money does not even reach the people living on Ebeye; the local landowners largely funnel it off-island. This is a case of a small local elite being bought off while the rest of the local population is left to struggle with the consequences of dispossession caused by the U.S. military activities. This situation is hardly unique to Kwajalein. It is not uncommon for land- and business owners near military bases to benefit greatly from the military's presence and therefore to provide political support for militarization.

The amount of money the United States would need to spend to mitigate some of the consequences of missile defense testing on Kwajalein was referred to as "budget dust" by one resident I interviewed, especially when compared with the size of the missile defense testing program. And money is not the only issue. There are more intangible impacts of the military's use of Kwajalein: the sense of loss Marshallese feel due to their banishment from traditional lands, and the sense of humiliation that comes from being relocated against your will by a foreign power. The residents of the islands do not have any effective means to redress their grievances or much of a chance to have a say over the future of their homeland and the future of the missile range that has been placed in their midst. If they did, that would introduce democracy and self-determination into a situation that currently lacks both. These notions, which are trumpeted loudly in the rhetoric of U.S. foreign policy, are absent from sites outside the gates of the Baseworld like Ebeye Island.

This examination of the missile defense program at Kwajalein demonstrates how the U.S. government has behaved (and continues to behave) in its military colonies. Although it would be much more difficult today for the U.S. government to relocate an entire population of an area on the U.S. mainland, move them onto a small prisonlike islet, and then fire missiles over it, we should ask why the government seems to have no problem behaving this way in other places like the military quasi colony of the Marshall Islands. Obviously the U.S. government has a different standard of conduct in the places it controls around the world than at home.

The Local Geographies of Bases in Places

It is important to know the story of Kwajalein not only because of the great suffering occurring on Ebeye but also because it is a story that is far from unique. The development of the missile defense program has negatively affected other Pacific sites, such as the west shore of Kauai island in Hawai'i (Barking Sands Pacific Missile Range Facility) and Jeju Island off the southern tip of South Korea (see map 2 in chapter 1), where construction of a new base for hosting missile defense "Aegis" destroyers began in 2011. Of course, missile defense operations are only one kind of military program affecting Pacific islands. Scattered throughout the region are training facilities, bombing ranges, and bases of various types that all have their own raison d'être. What many of them share in common, however, are histories of dispossession, abuse, colonialism, and contamination.

Case studies of places like Kwajalein demonstrate that living next to one of these facilities can be socially and environmentally degrading. In regard to negative impacts, the locations where the network of the U.S. military touches the ground have many similarities. First, on bases the day-to-day operation of the military negatively affects the local environment and the health and safety of people who live there. Second, because of these negative impacts, the military has repeatedly displaced local populations in host communities and has also taken advantage of, and helped perpetuate, the political colonization of these spaces.

In this sense military bases are doubly sites of violence. Rachel Woodward (2004) has emphasized that battlefields are but the "tip of the pyramid" of a vast (and expensive) complex that enables military activity. She examines these geographies of militarism as "the shaping of civilian space and social relations by military objectives, rationales and structures, either as part of the deliberate extension of military influence into civilian spheres of life and the prioritizing of military institutions, or as a byproduct of those processes" (Woodward, 2005, p. 721). As she highlights in her approach to understanding the network of military installations and institutions, "Armed conflict is only possible if a whole host of things fall into place" (Woodward, 2005, p. 727). Bases are not just sites for the production and global projection of military power and violence, however. They are also zones of encounter between the military and the people and environments that host them, and they are therefore the sites of a number of local, everyday violences (Enloe, 1990, 2000; Lutz, 2002).

At the outset of this discussion I should be clear about how I use the terms *militarism* and *militarization*. As Catherine Lutz (2002) contends, militarism is a "society's emphasis on martial values," while militarization "draws attention to the simultaneously material and discursive nature of military dominance" (p. 725). In other words, militarism is more a political philosophy while militarization is the concrete manifestation of military activity in place. Clearly the two are linked, but my focus is on the reshaping of host communities by *militarization*.

The militarization of communities has several negative environmental and social effects. These can differ by the type of base (logistical base, combat training area, Marines vs. Air Force, etc.), the size of the base, how active operations at the base have been, and the level of integration of the base and its personnel into the surrounding community. Despite these variations, the literature on the effects of militarization on host communities shows a number of commonalities. Some of these could be seen as positive or negative depending on one's position in the host community, and some are viewed almost universally as negative. Commonalities range from economic and cultural changes within a community to environmental contamination and greatly increased levels of rape and sexual assault (Enloe, 2000). On the positive side, there is often a pronounced economic effect due to personnel spending money off base as well as, in some instances, personnel actually living off base (Warf, 1997; Lutz, 2001). Furthermore, jobs in construction, food preparation, cleaning, and other labor-intensive activities on bases may produce income for nonmilitary members of the host community. Business elites in host locations will often compete for the militarization of their communities because of the increased revenue possibilities for those in a position to capture it (landowners, construction companies, and individuals who sell goods and services desired by military personnel). While these effects are well documented around domestic bases (Lutz, 2001; Woodward, 2004), they also take place around overseas bases (Enloe, 1990; Gillem, 2007). These economic impacts are usually painted as benefits, but there are also negative economic impacts, such as increases in local housing prices due to military subsidies to service people and job competition from laborers from other areas.

Military activities at bases also have profound environmental impacts. Besides the impacts at weapons-testing areas like Kwajalein (and Bikini Atoll and Vieques, Puerto Rico, discussed in chapters 3 and 4 respectively), other kinds of military areas suffer environmental problems that range from excessive noise caused by aircraft, combat training, and practice bombing to the widespread contamination of sites both on and off base (Santana, 2006; Inoue, 2004; Seager, 1993). In fact, it is difficult to find a major military facility anywhere on the planet that is not being investigated for severe chemical or radiological contamination that frequently does not stay confined inside the base's perimeter.[1] Also, as I discuss more in the following chapters, an environmental issue emerging at closed military facilities is that the sites are being turned into "nature preserves" so as to allow the Department of Defense (DOD) to avoid paying for cleaning up contamination to a level safe for human habitation (J. S. Davis, 2007a; S. Davis, Hayes-Conroy, & Jones, 2007; Havlick, 2007; Krupar, 2007).

Communities hosting military bases are also frequently sites of high levels of physical and sexual violence (Enloe, 1990, 2000, 2007; Lutz, 2001; Seager, 1993; Inoue, 2004; McCaffrey, 2002). Whether in the Philippines, Okinawa, Puerto Rico, Hawai'i, or Europe, or even within the continental United States, an almost inevitable consequence of hosting a military base is an increase in the number of rapes and other crimes such as theft, assaults, and drunk driving. As an example, according to Okinawan Women Act Against Military Violence there were 4,784 serious crimes committed by U.S. service personnel *reported* in Okinawa between 1972 and 1995. These crimes frequently go unpunished, as "Visiting Forces Agreements" shield U.S. service members from being tried in local courts (C. Johnson, 2007). Compounding the negative effects of economic changes, environmental contamination, and sexual violence are the everyday reminders of the military's dominance in the local landscape: the guarded fences, the noise from jets overhead and combat exercises, and the boisterous groups of military personnel roaming off base in the evenings (Lutz, 2001).

The second point I want to bring up about communities hosting military bases is that these common violences are linked to common processes of displacement and political colonization. To put it simply, since many people do not want to live next to these kinds of activities, either people are forcibly moved to make way for military operations, or the rights of people to resist militarization are curtailed through political colonization. There is a mutually reinforcing relationship between colonialism and militarization. Places are colonized because they are good locations for military bases, and military bases are put in colonies because they are politically controlled spaces from which the bases can operate relatively free from political or social opposition (Aldrich & Connell, 1998; S. Davis, 2011).

In the Asia-Pacific region (and in the Indian Ocean, the Middle East, and the Caribbean as well), colonies are vitally important locations for the functioning of the U.S. system of military bases. First, I should emphasize that the United States has colonies. It did not just have colonies in the past, it has them today. While much has been said about the modern era as one of "postcolonialism," there is nothing "post" about any of the American colonies at the empires' edge in the Pacific. These are places subject to U.S. power but not granted its full political processes and protections. While many of these places are small in size, they are important because they are critical nodes in the global projection of American military power. Without colonially controlled places in the Pacific, there is nowhere to test missile defense systems, no global reach for American bombers, no bases to protect trade or counterbalance China, and no training areas for soldiers garrisoned overseas.

This process of colonialism and militarization is not an artifact of history or the fault of only one American political party. As residents in places across these colonized islands can attest, this pattern of military use and colonial relationships does not appear to be changing. There has been a remarkable consistency in the position of American colonies over the past century through both Democratic and Republican administrations. Today missile defense testing *still* occurs at Kwajalein Atoll in the Marshall Islands. Contaminated sites across the Pacific are *still* denied funding for adequate cleanup of radioactive and chemical contamination. Hawaiian land is *still* used for military maneuvers (and the U.S. government continues to push to open old bombing ranges, modernize and expand existing ones, create new ones, and do more exercises in the surrounding waters). Guam is *still* expected to see one of the largest increases in militarization since World War II as thousands of Marines and Air Force personnel are added to the small island in the coming decade.

It is important to understand what is going on in these places not only because they are militarily important but also because they are *contemporary* sites of human rights abuses, forced expulsions of populations, willful withholding of political rights and sovereignty, and widespread environmental contamination. The main reasons these areas continue to be denied full independence are their strategic value and the fact that they contain U.S. bases (Petersen, 1998). In turn, these islands have been the sites of intensive military activities that would be hard to conduct in the continental United States and increasingly difficult in other countries with political sovereignty. The painful irony is that the United States enacts this violent expropriation, destruction, and denial of full citizenship in the name of establishing peace, democracy, and liberty elsewhere (and to continue the irony, this is done through the use of violence).

The Global Geography of U.S. Military Bases

Keeping these local consequences in mind, the following discussion about the global network of military bases can be put into better context. Military planners, foreign policy analysts, politicians, and some international relations specialists may tend to speak about the global network of military bases as if the bases were disembodied points on a map, but serious analyses of the network must grapple with the fact that it is not only arrayed across space but also situated in places. It is now a given in the fields of economics, geography, and cultural studies that processes commonly referred to as "globalization" can operate globally only if grounded in particular locales (Harvey, 1990; Massey, 1994), but there has been less attention to the fact that military power functions in much the same way. The global network of American military power, controlled from key locales (the White House, the Pentagon, regional command centers, and bases), affects different places around the world in different ways.

When viewed from the global scale, what does this network of militarized places look like? Although some excellent analyses of global military operations recognize the importance of analyzing local impacts (see, for instance, Gerson & Birchard, 1991; C. Johnson, 2004, 2007; Lutz, 2009; Sandars, 2000; Vine, 2012), getting an accurate global overview of the base network is still very difficult. The network is an ever-shifting mosaic that is difficult to pin down precisely. For instance, a seemingly simple question like "How many foreign U.S. military bases are there in 2013?" has answers ranging from thirty-four to well over a thousand depending on a host of factors. These factors include how one defines *military*, how one defines a base, how one defines *foreign*, and how one defines whether a base is a U.S. base (Critchlow, 2005; C. Johnson, 2004, 2007; Vine, 2012). For example, some communications and spy bases are not directly under the DOD and thus are not technically "military." Some "bases" do not permanently house many U.S. troops but are essentially empty until needed. Some U.S. bases are hard to define as "foreign" because they have been placed in parts of the world with current or recent colonial statuses like Guam, Hawai'i, the Marshall Islands, the British Indian Ocean Territory, and Puerto Rico. Lastly, some foreign bases used by U.S. military personnel are not officially "U.S." bases because they are technically under the jurisdiction of the host nation or are run by private security contractors that support U.S. military objectives.

Because of these multiple difficulties of definition, it is hard to show a detailed list or map of the U.S. base network. Nevertheless, tracing its general, shifting geography is possible. Intellectual frameworks such as the Project for a New American Century's 2000 *Rebuilding America's Defenses: Strategies, Forces, and Resources for a New Century* and government documents such as the Integrated Global Presence and Basing Strategy in 2004, the 2005 U.S. Global Defense Posture Review, and the Quadrennial Defense Reviews (the latest in 2010) give some detailed strategies for administering the network of U.S. bases.

Without glossing over the important regional differences in the kind of attention the U.S. government directs at different parts of the world, suffice it to say that very few places left on the globe (or in its orbit) are deemed to be outside the interest and vision of American power. Consequently, the network of bases is global as well. Increasingly the network is designed to be a permanent infrastructure that allows military power to be shifted with post-Fordist efficiency from some sites to others "just in time" and according to perceived crises that challenge U.S. hegemony. For instance, in 2004 both former secretary of defense Donald Rumsfeld and deputy undersecretary Ryan Henry discussed the new base network while refusing to pinpoint geographically where they thought threats to the United States might be located. Henry commented only that the United States "strove to base forces in locations that supported flexibility and speed of response *to anywhere* in an unpredictable environment" (Critchlow, 2005, p. 8, emphasis added).

In the DOD's geographical imagination, presumably the whole world is an "unpredictable environment" and the U.S. military must be able to act everywhere. A base outside the continental United States is not for defending the territory of the ally where the base is located. Instead, bases are now conceptualized as jumping-off points for offensive operations, counterattacks, and protecting "vital systems" like trade routes and energy supplies. The 2004 Global Defense Posture Review was quite explicit about this fundamental shift. The report states, "*The United States can no longer expect our forward forces to fight in place*; rather, for most forward-stationed U.S. forces, their purpose is to undertake operations on short notice by deploying rapidly into near or distant theaters" (p. 6, emphasis in original). The DOD envisions constructing a flexible network of bases that can swell or contract in response to shifting threats. Ideally, the nodes of the network (bases) would not be created or decommissioned through time. Instead, the network would be stable and the amount of personnel and material at any given base would respond to the geography of the threat.

The general tripartite architecture of this emerging network consists of Main Operating Bases, Forward Operating Sites, and Cooperative Security Locations. Main Operating Bases, as the name implies, would permanently have large numbers of personnel, solid infrastructure, and training areas. These bases are scattered around the globe to give ample general coverage of the major regions of the world.

For other operations, however, the United States must have access to bases closer to the sites of conflict. Forward Operating Sites (FOSs) have small rotating staffs and pre-positioned materials that are ready to increase in size if necessary. Sometimes these are referred to as "light-switch operations" because large numbers of troops can arrive and all they have to do is "turn on the lights" to start operating (Garamone, 2005). Camp Bondsteel in Kosovo, which hosts thousands of American military personnel, is an example of an expanded FOS.

Cooperative Security Locations (CSLs) are facilities with very small numbers of personnel (or none) that can be made usable on short notice. Also, these are often not technically "American" facilities, a technicality that gives them political cover in localities where there may be resistance to an American presence. Commentator Robert Kaplan (2005) described CSLs this way:

> Often the key role in managing a CSL is played by a private contractor. In Asia, for example, the private contractor is usually a retired American noncom, either Navy or Air Force, quite likely a maintenance expert, who is living in, say, Thailand or the Philippines, speaks the language fluently, perhaps has married locally after a divorce back home, and is generally much liked by the locals. He rents his facilities at the base from the host-country military, and then charges a fee to the U.S. Air Force pilots transiting the base. Officially he is in business for himself, which the host country likes because it can then claim it is not really working with the American military. Of course no one, including the local media, believes this. But the very fact that a relationship with the U.S. armed forces is indirect rather than direct eases tensions. (p. 4)

This is not only Kaplan's view of CSLs. Former undersecretary of defense Ryan Henry (2006) also approvingly quotes Kaplan at length in his analysis of the contemporary global base network. Furthermore, this base architecture may have been a child of the Bush Doctrine, but as others have shown, it has been thoroughly endorsed and furthered by the Obama administration (Lutz, 2009; Vine, 2012).

Within this three-level structure of bases, the decision of which bases to enlarge and which to shrink depends on the judgment of the Pentagon and White House according to American grand political-economic strategies and their geopolitical vision of the day. There is, however, another important factor that shapes the U.S. base network: resistance. This resistance comes in the form of popular protests against these bases as well as in the form of political restrictions the U.S. military feels it may be subjected to in foreign territory. As I describe more fully in chapter 4, these resistances have been widespread and often successful.

In the following chapters I examine some other contemporary U.S. military colonies to show that the U.S. project of maintaining hegemony in Asia and the Pacific continues to be made possible by a way of operating in place based on injustice, environmental destruction, and planned misery. I also show how activists living in these places actively, and sometimes quite successfully, resist the entwined curse of militarization and colonialism. In this vein, one of my primary motivations for writing this book is to present information about these many sites because I think it is vital for people to have a deeper understanding of the current colonial apparatus so that they can have informed discussions about the costs and benefits of American foreign policy. In the dozens of times I have given my lecture about Kwajalein, often in front of more than a hundred students at a time, I recall only a single college student who had ever heard of Kwajalein and understood what goes on there. The geography of small islands in the Pacific is not exactly every college student's expertise, but the more classes I taught, the more I realized that almost *nobody* knew much about what occurs at sites crucial to U.S. foreign policy. Kwajalein was not the only unfamiliar place. The geographies and histories of Bikini Atoll, Diego Garcia, Okinawa, Guam, Hawai'i, Puerto Rico, Iraq, and Afghanistan were virtually unknown.

While the lack of knowledge about these sites has been somewhat disheartening, I have enjoyed giving these lectures because the responses to them have been strong. Once I complete my discussions of the history and present of one of these sites, students almost universally express surprise and outrage. Furthermore, they are incredulous as to why they had never heard about these situations before. I vividly remember one student who asked me after a discussion of missile defense testing and its effects on Kwajalein, "How in the world can the U.S. government justify what they are doing?" My response at the time, which I think is still accurate, was that the government does not have to come up with a justification if people simply don't know about it. I then referred back to the fact that in an auditorium of college students, nobody had ever heard of the place, let alone its militarized history and present. I argue that the obscurity of these crucial places for U.S. foreign policy is not an accident; it is largely a result of purposeful omission and outright discursive erasure of the lives of people who live on these islands. This book is an attempt to reverse this tactic by presenting the stories of these places and to enhance the political possibilities those stories can create.

CHAPTER 3

Seeing like an Empire

Islands as Wastelands

In this chapter I examine a particular aspect of how the United States attained and maintains its hegemonic status in the world: the development of nuclear weapons. To do so, however, I continue pursuing the book's theme of examining how colonialism, militarization, and the destruction of Pacific landscapes have operated in concert to enable the production of U.S. hegemonic power. To continue that theme, in this chapter I examine the discursive representation and physical destruction of Bikini Atoll. The indigenous population of Bikini, also located in the Marshall Islands (see map 3 in chapter 2), was removed by the U.S. military in 1946 to make way for twenty-three nuclear bomb detonations between 1946 and 1958. I am trying to do two things by telling the story of this site. First, I wish to describe in detail how the U.S. military apparatus legitimizes the takeover and destruction of island environments by deploying a particular, imperial way of seeing places. Second, I want to show how the representations of these places, and the myths of uselessness and disposability that are created, have very real material effects on landscapes and the bodies of people that call them home (Shields, 1991; Wright, 2006). Furthermore, this way of seeing and representing islands is repeated in militarized colonies across the region to the present day.

The colonization and military use of Bikini Atoll is a foundational story of how U.S. military institutions came to view the landscapes and islands under their jurisdiction during the formative years of America's post–World War II rise to global hegemony. My goal here is to look more closely at *how* the processes of colonization and militarization construct "bare life," and how they recast colonized places as "disposable." I want to give readers a sense of how other contemporary U.S. military colonies are *still* being constructed both in the discursive/imaginative sense and in a physical/material manner.

To begin my discussion of representations of the atoll, I begin with my own. Before I visited Bikini Atoll for the first time in 2001, I had already been exposed to hundreds of representations of the place.[1] I had read scholarly and popular written accounts of its history of nuclear testing. I had seen hours of documentaries depicting the military presence on the island and footage of Bikinians collecting their belongings and departing their homeland on Navy ships in 1946. I had looked at hundreds of photos of mushroom clouds towering over anchored Navy test ships and fireballs rising behind shivering palm fronds. So when I got to Bikini, I already carried a mental picture of what the place was like.

At least so I thought as I walked down to the beach at Bikini Atoll and stared out toward the sites of some of the most destructive explosions ever detonated. In a sweeping arc the white sand beach facing the lagoon extended outward in both directions. Lined with drooping pandanus and palm trees, the beach displayed only subtle hints of human habitation. From a flat rock on the beach I sat and looked out toward the spot in the lagoon where two atomic bombs, about the size of the bombs used against Hiroshima and Nagasaki (21 kilotons), were detonated in 1946 while the world watched the display of American power. I also looked at a spot on the horizon where the first deliverable hydrogen bomb was exploded on March 1, 1954. Code-named "Bravo," the bomb was 15 megatons—the largest bomb the United States ever detonated and nearly one thousand times as powerful as the bombs used against Japan. The bomb was so large that it spread deadly levels of radioactive fallout across the inhabited northern Marshall Islands before the radiation circulated in the high reaches of the atmosphere and deposited itself around the world.[2] The bomb also completely vaporized three islands on Bikini Atoll and left a mile-wide crater through the reef. Another indicator of the size of the Bravo bomb is that if a bomb of similar size were detonated over Washington, D.C., and the winds were blowing from the southwest, 90 percent of the populations of the District of Columbia, Baltimore, Philadelphia, and New York City would perish within three days. After the Bravo bomb, another twenty bombs, most of them hydrogen bombs, were detonated on and around Bikini Atoll throughout the 1950s. During the same time period, nearby Enewetak Atoll suffered forty-four such nuclear explosions.

As I stood on the site where many photos of the bomb blasts were taken, I looked out in the direction of these sites of tremendous violence. I stared out over one of the most abused lagoons in the world and tried to see evidence for what I knew had occurred. I looked for signs of destruction but found none. In a sense, I was looking for what I expected to see on the atoll. Looking for the expected is something, I argue, that many other actors (most more powerful than I) have done on this island as well. As I will discuss, many other visitors have come to Bikini thinking they knew what Bikini was before they ever set foot on it.

It has become axiomatic in scholarship on how we experience places that people tend to see in new places what they want or expect to see. What I want to explore in this chapter is not so much my experience with Bikini Atoll (which

FIGURE 4. The beach on Bikini. Photo by author.

is not all that exciting) or my perceptions of what Bikini Atoll is (which are not all that important). Rather, I am interested in how more powerful people and institutions have seen what they wanted to see on Bikini Atoll and the consequences of that visioning process. I refer to this visioning process as "Seeing like an Empire" to deliberately follow on James Scott's book *Seeing like a State: How Certain Schemes to Improve the Human Condition Have Failed* (1999). In his book Scott explains how governments have tended to view the lands under their domain as territories that need to be seen and managed from a central place. Scott argues that governments believe that in order to control the spaces they govern, they must arrange people and places to be visible. This visibility is often literal in the sense of having agents of the government able to see what resources exist in the realm, where people are, and what they are doing. To this end, governments—regardless of their purported leanings as democratic, fascist, socialist, or other—have developed elaborate apparatuses of control that most people living in modern societies take as facts of life: fixed and numbered addresses, unchanging legal names for their identities, monitored and policed public spaces, and standard weights and measures for resources. Scott argues that to facilitate this massive task of seeing their own country, centralized governments have actually changed and structured the very landscapes of the countries. Populations are encouraged or forced into nonnomadic lifestyles, and the resulting cities are aligned in grids so the state knows who is where. Even the trees of state forests are planted in lines so that they can more easily be inventoried and their status monitored by agents who have little knowledge of the local conditions that existed prior to the landscape's rearrangement into a "rational" order.

This way of transforming and "knowing" places is in contrast to Scott's description of how local people know their places. Unlike the government, which understands landscapes from afar in terms of population densities or available board-feet of trees, people living in landscapes tend to understand them quite differently. A dense forest viewed by a distant government as an impenetrable and unknowable morass (where its enemies can hide) may be known in quite detailed ways by the people living in it. People who have inhabited a landscape will generally have much more detailed knowledge not only about what is in it but also about the delicate interactions between themselves and that place. Furthermore, local people will attribute meanings to places in a very different way since those meanings are based on a lived experience. As landscape writer J. B. Jackson (1994) insists, the events we experience in a locality create our sense of place.

Local versions of place are not necessarily intrinsically superior or correct, but they are intrinsically very *different* from outsiders' views. Even if one valorizes local knowledge over the bureaucratic "view from afar," we should not fall into the racist trap that only certain types of people in the world (usually people thought of as primitive) have "local knowledge" and other, "modern" people have only "rational," colonialist knowledge. Everyone is local to somewhere, and everyone carries stereotypes of what places far away are like. What I want to explore in this chapter is how these local and nonlocal knowledges of place clash in these sites of the American Empire. In these places it is not just that views of place are different, but that the imperial view legitimizes the radical alteration and destruction of the place and the dispossession and forced removal of the inhabitants. These places are physically transformed to become "other-directed" landscapes that are restructured not according to the desires of the people who have lived in them, but according to the desires of people from afar (Hoelscher, 1998).

The vision that informs this transformation goes beyond Scott's "seeing like a state." The reason for labeling this colonial imagining process "seeing like an empire" is that there are some important distinctions. First, governmental institutions involved in colonial contexts are quite conscious that the lands they are contemplating changing are not their "own" lands, but the lands of others. As I noted in my discussion of "bare life" in the first chapter, the colonial context is somewhat different than the domestic sphere in that colonial landscapes are being managed by a state with the knowledge that the people who inhabit those landscapes do not belong to the protected "in-group" of citizens. I alter Scott's phrase to emphasize the colonial nature of these spaces because these landscapes are being seen—and being produced—explicitly as spaces inhabited by people the state is all too willing to sacrifice. I also use the phrase "seeing like an empire" to argue that what is going on in these places is a way of seeing employed not only by institutions of the government but also by individuals. The culturally encoded ways of seeing places affect a wide variety of actors from businesspeople to troops, tourists, and writers. They also affect people who become part of government institutions. While it is important to think about what imperatives institutions push onto the people who are part of them (especially the military), it is equally important to think about the ways of understanding the world that people bring with them into those institutions.

Much of the recent analysis of American foreign policy has focused on global power politics, the economic imperatives causing conflict over resources, or the linkages between these processes. What I want to do is to bring forward a perspective that has been somewhat buried by the focus on the global scale. Namely, I want to look at how people view places and how those views legitimize the often violent courses of action taken in American foreign policy. Rather than focus on the political or economic rationales behind empire, I want to look more closely at the cultural ones. The beliefs people have about places in the world, and about the people who inhabit these places, are powerful. On Bikini, dramatic differences between conceptualizations of place can highlight the more general *mechanisms* of dispossession and oppression occurring at colonial sites around the world. To make this case, in the remainder of the chapter I delve into some of the theories of how places are constructed and then apply the insights from this geographic research into my analysis of Bikini Atoll and other militarized islands. As I hope to show through this history, the consequences of imperial ways of conceptualizing places have been devastating.

Conceptualizing Places, Colonizing Places

In general, geographic theories of place emphasize four major points. First, nonlocal processes and events affect places (Massey, 1994). Second, different actors interpret places, create discourses about them, and thereby affect place reproduction (P. Jackson, 1989; Duncan & Ley, 1993; Casey, 2001). Third, meanings of places change through time, sometimes dramatically (Hall, 1997; McGuirk & Rowe, 2001). And finally, there is a dialectical interaction between spatial and social processes (Harvey, 1996; Soja, 1996; Cresswell, 2004). On the last point scholars have debated whether places are wholly constructed by social processes or the spatial and social are "mutually constitutive" (Cresswell, 2004, pp. 29–33). Bikini Atoll certainly is a place where all four of these points about place are readily apparent: external actors and discourses have had a heavy impact, interpretations of the place vary widely, those interpretations have transformed through time, and it is quite easy to see how the landscape and social processes have mutually constituted each other. While what happened on Bikini is somewhat hidden across large parts of the atoll's land- and seascape, we can also understand the atoll's history by looking at representations of the place.

Representations of place come in many forms. To name but a few: postcards (Dunn, 1996; Waitt & Head, 2002), monuments (Hall, 1997), images (Rose, 2001; Echtner & Prasad, 2003), written accounts (M. L. Pratt, 1992; Hutt, 1996), and verbal statements (Cohen, 1995). What all representations share, however, is that they are means of transmitting certain conceptualizations of a place to other people. Since they emphasize some characteristics of a place at the expense of others, they are always incomplete "pictures" of place. These representations are also political. They "do work" by reinforcing conceptualizations of a place that legitimize certain uses and prohibit others. In turn, the new form of the landscape informs new conceptualizations. This cyclical process is the essence of Henri Lefebvre's scholarship on the relationship between conceptualizations of places and landscape. He writes, "In actuality each of these two kinds of space [the physical and the imagined] involves, underpins and presupposes the other" (Lefebvre, 1991, p. 14). The fact that the reproduction of the landscape is entwined with imagined conceptualizations of the place leads to multiple, often contradictory, imaginings for a single physical landscape and can lead to conflicts and contests over how a place is constructed. Each individual has a different conceptualization of what a given place is (or ought to be), and the reproduction of the place is a social process. Places, therefore, are more than just the amalgam of the local inhabitants' imaginings; they are the result of spatially wide-ranging regimes of power and the ability of some individuals to legitimize one imagining of a place over others.

How, then, do people interpret a given landscape like Bikini Atoll in different ways? One way to examine this process is through the concept of "discursive-material formations," which draws together the trends in place research that recognize places as fluid, permeable, and affected by the ways in which they are imagined. While Lakshman Yapa has used the concept of discursive-material objects in his discussions of poverty and scientifically engineered seeds, I believe the concept can be extended to studies of place reproduction (J. S. Davis, 2005a; Yapa, 1996). Talking about places as discursive-material formations highlights the role of conceptualizations and representations of place in enabling and legitimizing certain versions of place over others. In terms of place reproduction, this perspective emphasizes that the way places are known, discussed, and represented through language legitimizes the performance of certain activities in those places and also directs the social practices that actively shape the landscape.

Roland Barthes's discussion of denotations and connotations can make this process clearer. The idea of denotation is that there is one true "real" meaning for a place or object. The idea of connotation suggests that there are multiple meanings available to link a word to a place or object. Barthes argues that there are always multiple meanings and that "denotation" is merely an ideological construct that aims to convince people that there is only one true meaning. He states, "Denotation is never anything more than the most attractive and subtle of connotations" (quoted in Baudrillard, 1981, p. 158). The theory of discursive-material formation hinges on this idea that there are multiple connotations available for any place or object. There is no one "true" meaning of a place. Rather, a person constructs a conceptualization of a place by noticing some of its attributes and attaching to it some of the available meanings (connotations) and disregarding other potential meanings. In other words, the place is not experienced wholly but through subsets of its attributes. It is not the "whole brute presence of place" that inscribes itself on people, but only the conceptualizations of it that last (Casey, 2001, p. 688). When interacting with a place, through either direct experience or a representation, a person notices only a few of its qualities; attributes unnoticed by one person may make a strong impression on another. People find meaning in a place not by accessing a "true" denotation but by finding a connotation based on what they are predisposed to look for. Through this process, people develop simplified readings of what a place means. In terms of Bikini Atoll, the military was looking for a place to perform nuclear experiments to bolster U.S. power, and they reduced the place to the characteristics they were seeking. Rob Shields (1991) describes this process as the construction of "place-images": "Such *place-images* come about through over-simplification (i.e., reduction to one trait), stereotyping (amplification of one or more traits) and labeling (where a place is deemed to be of a certain nature). Places and spaces are hypostatized from the world of real space relations to a symbolic realm of cultural significations. . . . These images connected with a place may even come to be held as signifiers of its essential character" (p. 47, emphasis in original).

Shields goes on to argue that sets of place-images with particular coherence and longevity coalesce into what he refers to as "place-myths." The use of the term *myth* here is not meant to imply that the conceptualization of place is somehow opposed to the "real facts" about a place, but rather that there is a coherence to the imaginings along a certain culturally significant theme. Place-myths, while shifting somewhat as a landscape changes, have a permanence and inertia that are often slow to change. What is more important for my purposes is that multiple and contradictory place-myths can exist for the same place at the same time and that these myths can shift through time. Shields (1991) writes, "Opposed groups may succeed in generating antithetical place-myths (as opposed to just variations in place-images) reflecting different class experiences or the cultural remembrance of a defeat where conquerors see only glory" (p. 61). Bikini Atoll, like other military islands, has been shaped by actors who have conceptualized the place using very different attributes than those emphasized by many of the Bikinian people. As a result, conflicts occur over which physical attributes and social practices on Bikini are to be celebrated and enhanced and which are to be vilified and erased.

This discussion of place conceptualization still leaves open the question of how these varied imaginings entwine with social practices to reproduce the material landscape. It is important not to see the discursive-material concept as suggesting that words build houses or discourses drop bombs. Using the language of discursive-material formations does not imply that discourses telekinetically transform reality or that the landscape does not exist prior to our views of it. What it does demonstrate is that the concepts enabling and legitimizing the material reproduction of place originate not from an unmediated perception of a material landscape, but from the various conceptualizations of that landscape, mediated by discourses that are often quite independent from the materiality of that place.

Furthermore, it is critical to note that place-images and place-myths are often *pre-established*. In other words, conceptualizations of a particular place, like the conceptualizations I had of Bikini Atoll, are often formed *before* a place is directly experienced. The imagined landscape of a place often comes not just from the sensory experience of that particular environment, but from the semiotic linking of that experience to previously known places, cultural narratives, and meanings. So the imagined landscape is not only a product of the material landscape, it is a melding of the material landscape with images of *other* places. The sensory experience in the landscape is not the sole source for the meaning of a place, but only one of the sources. The pre-established place-images mesh with sensory experiences of place to create floating signifiers: culturally available traveling conceptualizations of places that do not arise from a particular place as much as they are applied to it.

To sum up, discourses and place-images that emanate from far outside the physical place affect how a place is conceptualized. The place-myth generated for a given site may have much more to do with stories and images of other places deemed to be "like" it than with the landscape of the place itself. The island Pacific is certainly one region where Western place-myths have been constructed throughout history based on the islands' antipodal position to Europe, biblical searches for Eden, and Rousseau's romanticism (Jolly, 1997; Howe, 2000).[3] Such traveling place-myths then land on specific islands and are applied with little concern for the specific materiality or social conditions of that place. The place-myth of the "deserted isle" has been applied to their atoll despite the fact that the Bikinian people have lived there for generations (and still desire to live there). Bikini Atoll has *become* a "deserted isle" by the linking of Bikini's material environment with narratives that have been constructed in Western culture over thousands of years in a wide variety of geographic contexts. In turn, place-myths enable and legitimize social practices that alter the material landscape and attempt to bring it more into line with a conceptualization that was never based on the original landscape in the first place.

Bikini as Home and as Ideal Sacrifice Area

In 1946 Bikini Atoll was not "found" as an ideal test site; it was made into one. Two quotes exemplify this position. First, Denis Cosgrove (1998) said of nuclear test sites, "The 'hole in the map' was a pre-condition for a nuclear hole in the ground; it alone created the necessary marginality for experimentation to be deemed acceptable" (p. 264). Specifically referring to Bikini, a commentator in the 1970s referred to the selection of the atoll as a test site this way:

> Bikini had been, after all, a place of human habitation, a homeland. When the atoll was acquired by the U.S. Navy it had about 150 inhabitants. It had, however, something even more important: geography. The trifling life of the little island could not reasonably share in a transcendental experience that was, when all was said and done, dedicated to death. The whole function of Bikini was to be remote, far away, as inaccessible as possible from anything valued by man, because it was to be destroyed. . . . A place had to be found where the principle of overkill could be examined, where nuclear bombs could be tested in the atmosphere without inconveniencing anyone, at least anyone much. The Micronesian people of the central Pacific are by definition nobody much. (Cameron, 1970, p. 24)

Before nuclear testing, Bikini was considered a healthy homeland by its inhabitants, who had lived on the atoll for generations (Niedenthal, 2001). It was a place with ample land and adequate fishing resources. It was the location of the graves of the Bikinians' ancestors. The U.S. military, however, emphasized a very different set of attributes.

The first atomic tests at Bikini in 1946 served several purposes for the U.S. military. On a geopolitical level the testing acted as a theater in which the

United States could openly demonstrate the power of their atomic arsenal. In contrast to the secrecy surrounding atomic experimentation during World War II, the tests at Bikini were highly publicized. Representatives from many countries were invited to witness the tests as a demonstration of American military power.[4] The military's primary stated purpose for the first set of tests at Bikini in 1946, however, was more practical. The tests were conducted jointly by the Army and Navy amid debate in the American military over whether atomic weapons had made the Navy obsolete. The tests were designed to determine whether naval vessels could withstand atomic attack (Weisgall, 1994). This rivalry between the two branches of the armed services figured prominently in the underlying rationale for the tests, code-named "Operation Crossroads" because, as the admiral in charge of the tests noted, "seapower, airpower, and perhaps humanity itself are at the crossroads" (quoted in Weisgall, 1994, p. 32).

The plan was to anchor an armada of captured German and Japanese naval vessels, as well as older American ships, in a lagoon and then explode atomic bombs near them. The first test was to be an air-dropped bomb, the second bomb was to be exploded underwater, and a third test was to involve an even deeper underwater detonation. The first two tests were carried out in the summer of 1946, but the deep underwater detonation was cancelled. In the end, the "contest" between the Navy and Army was seen as a draw. Most of the ships used in the tests were sunk or unusable after the tests.[5] The Navy-delivered underwater bomb blast, however, was credited with doing much more damage to the fleet than the Army's air-dropped bomb.

So how was it that Bikini, an inhabited island, became the site for these tests? Since the tests required a site that accommodated the anchorage of large ships, continental sites imagined as remote by the U.S. government, such as New Mexico and Nevada, could not be considered. While the first atomic bomb test had occurred in New Mexico in 1945, the discovery of serious radioactive contamination following the bombing of Hiroshima and Nagasaki caused the U.S. government initially to be cautious about conducting further atomic tests in or near the continental United States.[6] The Atomic Energy Commission therefore suggested that the Operation Crossroads tests be performed "overseas" (Weisgall, 1994, p. 31). In October 1945, two officers in the Navy's OP-06 office of special weapons, Frederick Ashworth and Horacio Rivero, stated, "We just took out dozens of maps and started looking for remote sites. After checking the Atlantic, we moved to the west coast and just kept looking" (quoted in Weisgall, 1994, p. 32). In December 1945, Ashworth said, referring to the search for the site, "We haven't come to any particular conclusion. It looks like *pretty far away* is going to be the answer" (quoted in Weisgall, 1994, p. 32, emphasis added). The searchers soon determined that the only places "pretty far away" were located in the Pacific. Bikini was selected over other sites in the Marshall Islands, Caroline Islands, and even the Galapagos Islands. William Pratt, a retired U.S. navy officer, summed up the requirements in his short 1946 article "How Bikini Became the Bomb-Testing Ground." He characterizes Bikini as "the ideal place" because of its location in a part of the world controlled by the United States; its relative freedom from tropical storms; its sheltered lagoon sizable enough to hold a naval fleet; and the atoll's small population (W. Pratt, 1946, p. 60). In addition, the atoll itself could be used as a staging area for the tests, as could the nearby American base at Kwajalein Atoll 240 kilometers to the south.

Bikini became the ideal *location* for a test site due to its remoteness from parts of the world deemed important to the U.S. military. Once selected, however, the atoll needed to be characterized as marginal in other ways so that it could be conceptualized as an ideal *locale* for atomic explosions. The dominant myth that guided representations of the atoll was that of the "deserted isle." Two similar but distinct kinds of representations were used to portray Bikini Atoll as a place worthy of nuclear destruction. In one sense it was represented as a "nonplace." In other instances, it was portrayed as a place that represented "backwardness": the antithesis of the Americans' technological modernity. No doubt both of these representations draw heavily on the mythology of the deserted isle, and both serve to legitimize the use of Bikini as a test site. I think, however, it would be a mistake analytically to completely fuse the two.

In regards to empty "nonplaces," Henri Lefebvre (1991) writes, "The notion of a space which is at first empty, but is later filled by a social life and modified by it, also depends on this hypothetical initial 'purity,' identified as 'nature' and as a sort of ground zero of human reality. Empty space in the sense of a mental and social void which facilitates the socialization of a not-yet-social realm is actually merely a representation of space" (p. 190). It is worth looking closely at what Henri Lefebvre is saying in this quote because I believe it is critical for understanding how "seeing like an empire" works. Essentially, Bikini was seen as an "empty space" on which the United States could conduct its military activities. The point Lefebvre is making is that there are not really many empty spaces in the world. Rather, places are often *represented as such for political ends*—a standard operating procedure of empires. In the seventeenth and eighteenth centuries, North America and its millions of native inhabitants were deemed to be "nature" and therefore available to European colonists. Australia was labeled "Terra Nullius," allowing the British to take possession of the legally empty land. More recently places like Iraq, Afghanistan, Palestine, and post-Katrina New Orleans have been portrayed as "blank slates" for grand economic or social projects.[7]

This mental conceptualization of Bikini as an empty "nonplace" is rooted in prior U.S. conceptualizations of the entire Micronesian region as a nonplace (Steinberg, 2001). The atoll was assumed to be but a minor blemish on an ocean surface regarded by Americans in World War II as a nonplace. This portrayal of atolls is demonstrated by reference to the islands as mere "anchored aircraft carriers."[8] One U.S. official described the atolls of the Marshalls this way: "Living on an atoll is like living on a ship, except that the ship will get to port, but the atoll will never go anywhere" (quoted in Weisgall, 1994, p. 35). This portrayal of Bikini as terra nullius presaged the selection of future places considered for nuclear testing sites from Maralinga, Australia, to central Pennsylvania (Pilger, 1989; Krygier, 1998).

One difficulty with portraying Bikini as a deserted isle was that the Bikinians lived there. This fact, however, only necessitated a different strategy of representation. To show that the inhabited atoll was "actually" a nonplace, the atoll had to be portrayed as unhealthy and the people that inhabited the atoll had to be seen as removable. A U.S. Navy admiral proclaimed that "the atoll itself is unhealthy" because it "produce[d] little food besides coconuts and fish" (W. Pratt, 1946, p. 60). This comment served to delegitimize the existence of the Bikinians on the atoll and to suggest that they would be better off somewhere else.

Early in 1946, the Bikinians were moved to nearby Rongerik Atoll. While the United States had made the decision months earlier to use Bikini as a test site, representatives of the Navy, in front of newsreel cameras, made a ceremony of asking the Bikinians to leave their atoll. The Navy knew that the Bikinians had been Christianized in the early 1900s, and the military governor of the Marshalls persuaded the Bikinians to leave by comparing the Bikinians to the children of Israel (Kiste, 1974, p. 27). According to anthropologist Leonard Mason:

> In February of 1946, Commodore Ben H. Wyatt, the military governor of the Marshalls, traveled to Bikini and, in a Sunday after church, assembled the Bikinians to ask if they would be willing to leave their atoll temporarily so that the United States could begin testing atomic bombs for "the good of mankind and to end all world wars." King Juda, then the leader of the Bikinian people, stood up after much confused and sorrowful deliberation among his people, and announced, "If the United States government and the scientists of the world want to use our island and atoll for furthering development, which with god's blessing will result in kindness and benefit to all mankind, my people will be pleased to go elsewhere. (quoted in Niedenthal, 1997, p. 30)

The word that best describes the time between the decision and the actual relocation of the Bikinians is "spectacle." A *National Geographic* article published in 1946 describes how the last month of the people living on Bikini was one long staged photo opportunity for reporters and filmmakers.[9] The final

Bikinian church service was performed three times so cameras could get different angles, and the Bikinians were often repositioned for effect or to cover microphones. The articles and newsreels created from this period helped cement the idea in the world's imagination that the Bikini Islanders were primitive, Christianized, loyal subjects sacrificing themselves to the greater good of the United States.

The U.S. military used the imagined cultural inferiority of the Bikinians and their supposed weak attachment to Bikini to legitimate the Bikinians' removal from their atoll. Here we see another place-myth emerge regarding Bikini. The focus is on Bikini as a marginalized place rather than on its "nonplace" attributes. Marginalization, as the word implies, suggests that Bikini was a place of some sort but antithetical to what existed in the imagined "center." Rob Shields (1991) contends that "to be 'on the margin' has implied exclusion from 'the center.' But social, political, and economic relations bind peripheries to centers, keep them together in a series of binary relationships, rather than allowing disconnection. In this way, 'margins' become signifiers of everything centers deny or repress" (p. 276).

The portrayal of Bikini and the Bikinians as the primitive opposite of the progressive Americans is illustrated by the title of an article in the *New York Times Magazine* in 1946: "The Strange People from Bikini: Primitive they are, but they love one another and the American visitors who took their home" (Rooney, 1946). The view of the Bikinians as "simple primitives" is echoed in a *National Geographic* article that opens, "about the middle of February, 1946, modern civilization suddenly overtook the natives of Bikini Atoll" and closes with the thought, "Civilization and the Atomic Age had come to Bikini, and they [the Bikinians] had been in the way" (Markwith, 1946, pp. 97, 116). A newsreel informed American viewers about the Bikinians' removal from their island by claiming, "The islanders are a nomadic group, and are well pleased that the Yanks are going to add a little variety to their lives" (quoted in Weisgall, 1994, p. 162). Furthermore, many Americans involved with the tests viewed the removal of the Bikinians to nearby Rongerik Atoll as an even trade, if not an improvement in the Bikinians' condition. In their imagination, the periphery was the periphery and an atoll was an atoll. As E. J. Rooney (1946) wrote, "Bikini and Rongerik look as alike as two Idaho potatoes" (p. 25).[10]

On Bikini, as in most places, one group's imagined periphery is another group's imagined center. As would be expected from a group of people with generations of experience in a place, most Bikinians held very different views than the American military regarding both their home atoll and Rongerik Atoll, where they were forced to relocate. Many Bikinians regarded Bikini Atoll as a homeland rich in resources, the site of their lived experiences, and a cultural landscape saturated with meanings, deities, and the graves of their ancestors (Niedenthal, 2001). The traditional Bikinian stories regarding Rongerik, which is one-sixth the size of Bikini, portray it as a form of hell where a demon named Litobora left the fish, coconuts, and pandanus trees poisoned.

Two months after the Bikinians arrived on Rongerik, water and food supplies were found to be inadequate, and the people began requesting repatriation to Bikini ("Atomic age," 1946). Their requests were largely ignored by the U.S. Navy. The Navy was apparently unaware that the Bikinians were suffering from starvation and symptoms matching ciguatera (a type of poisoning from contaminated fish) until anthropologist Leonard Mason visited the atoll in 1948 (Kiste, 1985; Niedenthal, 2001). At the urging of Mason, the U.S. government moved the Bikinians from Rongerik to a camp next to an airstrip on Kwajalein. A year later, they were moved to Kili Island in the southern Marshall Islands (Kiste, 1974). Kili is a single, isolated island approximately 200 acres in size—approximately one-ninth of the land area of Bikini Atoll—with no lagoon. Over one thousand Bikinians live there today. One Bikinian described Kili Island this way: "At Bikini, one could always go to another island, but here it's always the same. Sleep, wake up, Kili. Sleep, wake up, Kili. Again, sleep, wake up, Kili. Kili is a prison" (quoted in Weisgall, 1980, p. 83).

In 1946, Bikini Atoll was conceptualized in many different ways. While the clear divide between "American" and "Bikinian" conceptualizations of Bikini is reasonably obvious, setting up a dichotomy between the two is too simplistic. We should not forget that there were differences in the way the atoll was conceptualized within each of these groups. Most notably, there was widespread disapproval in the United States over using Bikini as an atomic test site as well as lamentation on the part of Americans on Bikini that the atoll was going to be damaged by nuclear testing (Weisgall, 1994). In the end, however, the conceptualization of Bikini as a marginal "deserted isle" enabled the U.S. military to legitimize the explosion not only of the initial two atomic bombs on Bikini in 1946, but another twenty-one much larger hydrogen bomb blasts over the next twelve years.[11]

Radioactive Wasteland or Safe Home?

After the initial tests at Bikini, the island faded from the world's consciousness while the bathing suit that bears its name became the most popular connotation of the word. Introduced in 1946 by French designer Louis Reard, the bikini bathing suit was named after the atoll due to the intense media attention that Bikini received during Operation Crossroads. Allegedly, the "effects wrought by the scantily clad woman" in a bikini swimsuit were compared with the impact of the atomic bomb (Cameron, 1970, p. 26).[12] While the popularity of the swimsuit caused worldwide identification of the word "bikini" with the swimsuit and not the atoll, the atoll itself once again made news in the mid-1950s when the testing of hydrogen bombs expanded from nearby Enewetak Atoll to Bikini.

As mentioned, of the hydrogen bomb tests performed on Bikini from 1954 to 1958, test shot "Bravo," on March 1, 1954, was the most destructive. A hydrogen bomb test nearly one thousand times as explosive as the bomb dropped on Hiroshima, Bravo vaporized three of the islands on the northern rim of the atoll and left a large crater through the atoll reef. The pulverized bits of coral landed as fallout over the Pacific and on nearby Rongelap Atoll, and a radioactive wave washed over Bikini, "killing off all animal life except one hardy variety of rats" (Trumball, 1982, p. 49). The damage from Bravo was so great that there are reports that the top American official in the Marshalls, Maynard Neas, warned Marshallese leaders, "If anyone breathes a word of this, they'll be shot before sunrise" (G. Johnson, 1980, p. 58).

There was also a direct human cost to the Bravo detonation. Many residents of nearby Rongelap received massive doses of radiation from Bravo and have continued to have health problems, particularly thyroid abnormalities, to the present day (Simon, 1997). The Rongelapese claim they were intentionally contaminated as part of a U.S. experiment, and there is substantial evidence to support that claim. The Japanese fishing boat *Daigo Fukuryu Maru*, which sailed into the area during the test, was also affected by fallout from Bravo. One person on board died from radiation poisoning. When the tuna the crew caught entered the market in Japan, a panic over "Bikini Tuna" arose (Weideman, 1954). The effects of the test were so significant that March 1 is now a national holiday in the Marshall Islands (Nuclear Victims' Day).

In 1958 the last nuclear test occurred at Bikini, and in the 1960s discourses about Bikini shifted from discussions of it as an ideal test site to discussions over how dangerous the atoll had become. Not only was the atoll radioactive, but it was littered with equipment and damaged facilities, and most of the coconut palms were gone (Diggs, 1969). The U.S. government promised the Bikinians that after the atoll was declared safe, people could move back. The United States tried to make the atoll habitable by clearing off debris and planting thousands of new palm trees. Using a high modernist style that is indicative of outsider-produced landscapes—a form of environmental management discussed at length by Scott (1999)—the trees were planted in eerily perfect rows across the island.

By the late 1960s, the U.S. government decided that the atoll was safe and repatriation could indeed begin. The scientific representations of Bikini had changed; one article referred to Bikini as a "renovated paradise" (MacDougall, 1974). However, the Bikinian Council, the local government for the Bikinians,

FIGURE 5. Replanted palm trees on Bikini. Photo by author.

voted not to return due to distrust of the reports that the atoll was safe. They said, though, that they would not prevent individuals from going on their own (Niedenthal, 2001). In the early 1970s, some Bikinians went back to the atoll. Tommy McCraw, a scientist with the American government, went with them and tried to convince them that the atoll was not radioactively hazardous. *Life* magazine reported on the Bikinians' return, as well as their distrust: "Farther down the beach we came upon a single, stunted coconut palm bearing stunted fruit. Two Bikinians were already there and had harvested some of the nuts and cut them open. On our arrival they held them out and asked if they were safe to drink. 'Sure,' said McCraw, 'they're good,' and he made a motion for them to drink. But they hesitated. One of them held his coconut out and made the same motion to McCraw. Laughing, he took the nut and drank from it till it was empty. The Bikinians laughed too and drank with confidence" (Mydans, 1968, p. 33). Five years later, medical doctors discovered that the bodies of the atoll's residents had ten times the safe level of radioactive cesium and four times the safe level of strontium (Simon, 1997). Scientists found that the radioactive contamination resulted largely from eating the coconuts. In 1978 those living on Bikini were once again expelled from their atoll. A Bikinian said of the experience: "[W]e really didn't have any worries until those scientists started talking about the island being poisoned again. . . . We were so heartbroken that we did not know what to do. . . . We were sad, but we didn't want to make a problem for the Americans. If they say move, we move" (Pero Joel, quoted in Niedenthal, 2001, p. 72).

Understandably, the past experiences of the Bikinian community affect their decisions regarding repatriation today. As of 2013 the atoll still does not host a permanent population even as surrounding atolls such as Enewetak and Rongelap have been cautiously resettled. At present, there are conflicting views regarding the safety of Bikini, and many Bikinians remain distrustful of scientific proclamations regarding the safety of the atoll. During my discussions with members of the Bikinian community, people often expressed frustration over the mixed messages they had received from different scientific reports. In particular, there was a strong reaction when the Bikinians discovered that the U.S. EPA standard for radiation in the United States is 15 millirems above background level, while 100 millirems above background level is considered safe for the Marshall Islands. The existence of this double standard for radiation exposure has served to erode the Bikinians' trust in scientific studies of safe levels of radiation. Due to the ambiguity about the atoll's current radiological safety, the atoll has actually become what the U.S. military envisioned it to be in the first place: a deserted island.

Beyond Bikini

While the story of what happened on Bikini Atoll is important in its own right, it is also a story with broader implications. I am presenting this history of Bikini not because it is exotic or exceptional, but because it depicts a particularly fluid and well-documented case of how place meanings are contested, shift through time, and affect people and landscapes across the Baseworld. On Bikini the U.S. military attempted to remake the place through social practices enabled and legitimized by the place-myth of the "deserted isle." The atoll was then reproduced and altered in ways that were dictated not by its location, its endogenous attributes, or its position in a global political economic system, but rather by how it had been conceptualized. These conceptualizations have been rooted not only in the landscape itself, but in a semiotic system of codes that relates what people see on Bikini with signs they have previously encountered in other places. People then act to reproduce the atoll according to these conceptualizations of place. On Bikini the U.S. military's way of "seeing like an empire" resulted in conceptualizations of place that legitimized the displacement of the inhabitants and widespread environmental destruction.

Bikini's story is an example of the destruction of a people and a place in the name of attaining and projecting hegemonic power. As quotes in this chapter show, military planners held to a place-myth that portrayed the atoll as an acceptable, even deserving, place of destruction. Led by the ethos that "to make an omelet you have to break a few eggs," Bikini and the security of its people were sacrificed for the sake of American national security and hegemony-seeking power.

Bikini is not the only site where this sort of sacrifice has been occurring. To stretch the omelet analogy a bit, we should consider why indigenous communities' eggs are continually the ones getting broken in order to make the U.S. military's breakfast. Clearly the arrogant approach of "seeing like an empire" is underpinned by an implicit racism that assumes that some people's places matter and other people's places, bodies, cultures, and environments do not matter at all (Agamben's "bare life" argument certainly applies here). This attitude has led to the complete destruction, or massive demolition and reorientation, of human and environmental landscapes across the world. Islands like Enewetak, Rongelap, Kwajalein, Guam, Vieques, Diego Garcia, O'ahu, Kaho'olawe, Tinian, Okinawa, and many others have suffered fates perhaps not as fully destructive as what occurred on Bikini, but enabled by a similar process of mythmaking, displacement, and physical obliteration. As I discuss in the coming chapters, this process is not just historical. In many places the imperial way of seeing that operated on Bikini informs projects that are still going on today.

CHAPTER 4

Local Resistances and Imperial Reactions

The imperial "way of seeing" described in previous chapters operates in many sites across the Baseworld, and numerous consequences stem from the associated militarization of island communities. First, the decision to locate bases in these places affects the islands' physical, biological, and social landscapes, with concomitant impacts on the well-being of the inhabitants and the islands' political statuses. Second, these negative impacts create local resistances that have had some major successes in altering the spatial arrangement of the global network of U.S. bases. Third, the military reacts to these resistances through regional maneuvering that includes the reinforcement of colonialism on Pacific islands. This chapter (along with chapter 5) presents some of the local geographical detail in order to set the stage for a discussion in the final chapter that examines how groups in these militarized spaces challenge the operation of hegemony and seek affinity in international politics.

Part 1: Repeating Islands of Militarization and Resistance

To begin, we should note that the imperial way of seeing Bikini Atoll described in chapter 3 was not invented there, nor did it stop there. Chronologically, nuclear testing on Bikini was a midpoint in the travels of the U.S. government's way of seeing its colonized islands. As the United States extended its colonial reach in the 1890s to support its pursuit of global hegemony, it began to establish a template for politically taking over and changing the landscapes of the islands it came to control. The use of similar strategies of appropriation and forced displacement, as well as the imposition of standard building techniques for U.S. bases, means that while islands like Guam, Tinian, Vieques, Diego Garcia, Kwajalein, Okinawa, and O'ahu are geographically isolated from each other—and have very different precolonial histories—there are uncanny similarities among these places. Not only are all of these islands sites of intense military use, they also are all nonsovereign territories that are either still in a direct colonial relationship with a metropolitan power (Diego Garcia and Guam), have been made into quasi-colonial, freely associated states or commonwealths (Kwajalein, Tinian, and Vieques), or have been previously independent nations absorbed by foreign powers (Hawaiʻi and Okinawa). Colonialism has stamped many of these places in the same way, and this is hardly surprising given how empires operate.

A useful way of characterizing the similarities across these far-flung islands can be found in Antonio Benítez-Rojo's (1997) theory of the "repeating island." In regard to imperial conceptualizations of islands, Benítez-Rojo focused on how Spanish colonialism remade each successive island in the mold of previously conquered islands. In this way, the islands' precontact landscapes were disregarded, recoded, and materially reproduced to suit imperial needs by a repeating Spanish colonial military/plantation machine. After the Spanish-American War at the end of the nineteenth century, the United States inherited many of these Spanish colonies and introduced their own pattern of repeating landscapes that suited the needs of their growing military and imperial ambitions. As Elizabeth DeLoughrey (2007) notes, expanding on Benítez-Rojo's concept, "the use of one archipelago as an ideological and social template for the next reveals the ways in which the colonial discourse of islands repeated itself, rhizomatically, along a westward trajectory" (p. 9).

It was not just colonial discourse that repeated itself, however. It was also the landscapes of militarization and colonial forms of domination that these discourses justified. These repeating landscapes of militarization were produced not just because a discourse demanded it but also because of the perceived threats posed by competing colonial projects. The Spanish Caribbean project was threatened by French, Dutch, and British colonialisms. On the Pacific edge of empires, the landscapes of militarization were shaped in the early part of the twentieth century by American, European, and Japanese colonialisms. The island Pacific has been heavily shaped by the rivalry between U.S. and Japanese power, with World War II arguably the most impactful event in Pacific history (Poyer, Falgout, & Carucci, 2001). While American and Japanese colonialisms are generally seen as competing projects, in many respects the two have worked in concert to construct the militarized and nonsovereign Pacific that we see today. This is because each colonial power tended to paint the islands as in need of defending against the other colonialism (Shigematsu & Camacho, 2010). After the end of World War II, a mutually reinforcing relationship continued to exist between military use and lack of sovereignty in the American-controlled Pacific, justified by the threat of first Soviet power and later Chinese power (Aldrich & Connell, 1998; Baldacchino, 2010). The result of this colonialist view is the repetition from island to island and archipelago to archipelago of a certain kind of militarized landscape dominated by similar types of military activities (i.e., the "Baseworld" described in chapter 2).

The problem with this repeating landscape of militarization is that it creates local environments full of hazards and annoyances to the people who live on these islands. Thus, many of these U.S. bases are surrounded by a ring of environmental advocates, community development activists, women's groups, health advocates, and others actively resisting the ways in which the violence the bases are meant to project elsewhere "leaks" into the surrounding community. While the various groups and movements resisting the inequities and violence around U.S. bases may have diverse foci such as issues of environmental contamination, sexual violence, or access to resources and land, they share a common concern for the everyday effects of the militarization of their places. In contrast to some organizations in the broader peace movement (Herb, 2005), these groups are born out of resistance to in-place violences to the bodies of activists, their families, and their communities. People living near bases may oppose various types of military operations, but one recurring theme has been local opposition to military training.

Maintaining large numbers of deployed military personnel means having the associated combat training areas. It is often these military training activities, and the large landholdings required for them, that lead to sustained resistance movements against the presence of U.S. bases in these "forward" places such as Japan, Guam, Hawai'i, and Puerto Rico. While training overseas has been a continually thorny issue for the military, strategic policy documents and proclamations by active duty commanders consistently declare that training areas, and the activities that go on in them, are absolutely essential parts of any large base (Calder, 2007; DOD, 2004; Gillem, 2007; Matthews, 2010). Following such dicta as "Every Marine is, first and foremost, a rifleman," the military steadfastly professes that military units *must* continue training even when deployed overseas. The military's insistence on conducting live-fire training, however, has led to lawsuits and some of the largest outpourings of antibase activism. Training at such areas as Makua Valley in Hawai'i and Farallon de Medinilla in the Northern Marianas has been blocked by environmental lawsuits, and other sites around the world have been permanently shut down (Kaho'olawe, Hawai'i, and Vieques, Puerto Rico). Others that remain open continue to serve as lightning rods for protest.

Even though the U.S. military has made a concerted effort to continue to represent these military colonies in accordance with the same Western cultural myth of the "deserted isle" that was applied to Bikini Atoll, people living on these islands have deployed counternarratives challenging this labeling of their islands as mere anchored aircraft carriers or repeating cogs in a military-colonizing, sovereignty-violating machine. The activities of the military, and the systems of colonialism put in place to support them, have sparked protest and resistance movements. The central themes in most of these movements are usually quite simple: First, there is the contention that military operations negatively affect the health, security, and well-being of people living on the islands and should be stopped. Second, there is usually a call for sovereignty and local control over politics.

Not only are the themes of this resistance similar across the Baseworld, but so are the strategies and tactics used by these movements. Thus, we can talk about another manner in which these places are "repeating islands": they are *repeating islands of resistance*. Benítez-Rojo's work is illustrative for examining this aspect of repeating islands as well. Benítez-Rojo, while looking at how colonial powers changed island landscapes to fit a repeating template, was also looking for explanations for the commonalities he saw among island cultures that seemed so splintered through colonial encounters. He looked at similarities across the Caribbean meta-archipelago and in its diasporas—commonalities shared among individuals despite different languages, colonial histories, ethnicities, politics, and current place of residence. Taking a self-described postmodern approach, he theorized that social life across the Caribbean islands and among its emigrants repeats itself in a fractal way. In other words, wider-scale social patterns are based on local practices that repeat and extend themselves across space, with small variations, from island to island and enclave to enclave. The emphasis here is not just on the repetition of the social patterns, but on the interconnectivity of islands. As the Tongan scholar Epeli Hau'ofa (1994) emphasizes, island communities are a "sea of islands" rather than islands in the sea. The sea is a connector, not the barrier it is imagined to be in colonial discourse. Islands are connected rhizomatically through the ocean, not despite of it. Or as poet and scholar Kamau Braithwaite puts it, "island unity is submarine" (quoted in DeLoughrey, 2007, p. 25).

This metaphor of the repeating island is illustrative for discussing the nature of antimilitary activism on these colonized islands. Even with very different geographies and histories, the homogenizing processes of militarization and colonialism have created common problems that are the basis for common solutions and affinity-seeking networks of solidarity. As I explore further in chapter 6, through these international networks activists share strategies and tactics, alert each other during times of crisis, regularly visit each other's communities (over great distances and at great expense), and sustain a decentralized global network of support. Before I delve into this network and the interconnections between these movements, however, I describe more fully the kinds of landscapes that exist on these islands and the local strategies and tactics of resistance they produce. I give examples of the situations on O'ahu, Hawai'i; Okinawa; and Vieques, Puerto Rico to demonstrate not only how "seeing like an empire" has created repeating islands of bases but also how the spirit of resistance repeats from island to island as well. My descriptions of these places are necessarily brief, but numerous other books give fuller accounts of militarization on these islands (see, for example, Ferguson & Turnbull, 1998; McCaffrey, 2002; Lutz, 2009; Shigematsu & Camacho, 2010; Ireland, 2010; McCormack & Norimatsu, 2012).

O'AHU, HAWAI'I

Staring down from the side of Halawa Heights Road next to the Marines' Camp H. M. Smith in Honolulu you get a panoramic view of the naval base at Pearl Harbor (a harbor traditionally known as Pu'uloa and renamed by the Americans). I was traveling around the island of O'ahu with members of a local antimilitarist organization dedicated to fighting both the militarization of the Hawaiian Islands and their political incorporation into the United States—an incorporation that was imposed on the islands in the wake of the 1893 overthrow of the Hawaiian Monarchy.[1] While Hawai'i is technically part of the United States and has greater access to the halls of political power than Guam or the Marshall Islands, the historically recent overthrow of its government, its long-term status as an American colony, and its huge military presence make it much more like other overseas military colonies than like the mainland of the United States.

We were touring militarized O'ahu. From the street next to Camp Smith I viewed the expanse of the naval installation that took over the harbor as my hosts pointed out the nearby airfields, the enormous X-band radar on an oil platform about to be shipped to the north Pacific for the missile defense program, and the large bunkers stocked with untold numbers of nuclear weapons. About a third of the island of O'ahu is occupied by military bases of one sort or another. It is a true military colony, and, like other military colonies, Hawai'i owes its political affiliation with the United States not to the riches it holds, but to its location relative to places of economic value. After Hawai'i was made into a U.S. territory, O'ahu became a stopover that allowed the United States to extend its reach to the western Pacific. The annexation of Hawai'i occurred in the late 1800s, when Manifest Destiny was being applied in the Pacific to the doorstep of Asia. In an era when European nations had already divided up the world among themselves, the United States needed a different strategy to bring

FIGURE 6. Pu'uloa Lagoon (aka Pearl Harbor). Photo by author.

wealth to its burgeoning capitalist economy once the age of conquest and expansion across the North American continent was coming to a close. American industrialists and politicians realized that to exploit Asia they did not need to possess colonies in Asia; they only needed to accumulate military colonies that enabled *access* to Asia.

This is the crucial difference between older forms of European *colonialism* and American *imperialism*. Colonialism is usually defined as direct control over a territory to enable the extraction of wealth from the area. Imperialism, in contrast, is usually defined as the *indirect* political and economic control over nominally "independent" territories to enable the extraction of wealth. The United States in the late 1800s had no need or ability to colonize the Asian mainland, only the need and ability to ensure access to it. So colonies were made of Hawai'i, American Samoa, Guam, and the Philippines. The latter two were wrested from the Spanish in the 1898 war when the United States also "freed" Cuba and gained Puerto Rico as a military colony to guard the approaches to Central America and the future Panama Canal. These new colonies were not substantially resource-rich colonies, but rather strategic locations that enabled a coal-using U.S. Navy to maintain a presence in the western Pacific, guard the route across the Pacific to Asian resources and markets, and deny other nations the same access.

The results of imperial decisions made since the late 1800s are littered everywhere across the Hawaiian landscape. Every branch of the military has facilities in Hawai'i. There are large air bases, such as Hickam Air Force Base and the Marine Corps Air Station at Kaneohe, as well as a huge naval complex at Pearl Harbor. There are also large training areas and bombing ranges around the islands. The whole island of Kaho'olawe, south of Maui, was bombed for decades until Hawai'i activists protested and managed to halt its use by the military. Makua Valley on O'ahu was used for live-fire training for over sixty years until forced to close in 2011. Neither Makua or Kaho'olawe, however, has been adequately cleaned or decontaminated. There are also active training areas: Pohakuloa on the Big Island, Schofield Barracks, and other locations. At present, the military footprint is not shrinking but expanding. In the early years of the twenty-first century the United States brought in new "Stryker Brigades" for training in the islands, a move that required the U.S. military to demand even more land.[2]

A drive around O'ahu easily demonstrates the heavy imprint of the military. From the fenced-off entrance to Makua Valley, to the giant naval communication antennae at Lualualei, to the Stryker Brigade training areas in the center of the island, to the ships crammed together in the West Loch of the naval base, to the stylish neighborhoods of housing for military families and the giant PX where military dependents shop: the military is ever-visible in the landscape (Ferguson & Turnbull, 1998). The military presence in O'ahu is more integrated into surrounding communities than it is in places like Kwajalein/Ebeye, but this has both positive and negative aspects. While there is less of a sharp disparity between the on-base and off-base landscapes, there is still plenty of difference. Furthermore, the leakage of military activities and personnel off the bases is more noticeable. The military uses civilian highways and roads, military planes abound in the skies, and all of the waters surrounding the Hawaiian Islands are open as areas for military training (even environmentally protected marine preserves like the huge Papahānaumokuākea Marine National Monument). Military personnel and their families also have a large and obvious presence on island, which, in addition to driving up housing costs, has environmental and cultural impacts. This militarization of Hawai'i has spawned active and effective resistance. As noted, training ranges in Makua Valley and Kaho'olawe have been closed because of sustained protests. These protests involved tactics ranging from lobbying, to sign holding and public rallies, to occupying and blocking access to the ranges. While such protests are not uncommon—and there is widespread support for antimilitary activism and associated calls for political sovereignty—there is also much support within Hawai'i for the perceived economic, political, and social benefits that militarization and incorporation into the United States have brought to the islands (Osorio, 2010).

OKINAWA

Like Hawai'i, Okinawa is a formerly independent place that has been absorbed by a larger power (see map 2 in chapter 1). Also like Hawai'i, it has almost a third of its land controlled by the U.S. military. Okinawa, the largest of the islands in the Ryukyu chain, was part of the formerly independent Ryukyu Kingdom, which was absorbed into the Japanese state in 1879. After invading Okinawa near the end of World War II, the United States administered Okinawa and the surrounding Ryukyu Islands until 1972, when the islands were transferred back to Japanese control. This formerly independent chain of islands suffers from what has been referred to as "double-colonization" by both the United States and Japan (Akibayashi & Takazato, 2009). Okinawa, while under Japanese political jurisdiction, hosts most of the American military forces in Japan. Since invading Okinawa at the end of World War II, the United States has kept extensive military assets there. Many members of the community see the numerous bases and training areas as threats to rather than protectors of their health and security. Areas near the bases have experienced helicopter crashes into the local university, pervasive jet noise, pollution, and crime (C. Johnson, 2007; Ueunten, 2010). Particularly tragic have been a number of well-publicized sexual attacks on Okinawan women and girls by U.S. military personnel, including a 1995 gang rape of a twelve-year-old. As mentioned, one Okinawan women's organization (Okinawan Women Act Against Military Violence) catalogued 4,784 reported serious crimes on island by American soldiers and sailors between 1972 and 1995.

Like Hawai'i, Okinawa has been a site of both intense militarization and effective antimilitary activism. The protests that have erupted in Okinawa due to these threats to local security have had an effect on the U.S. military's posture on the island. After protests increased in intensity in the mid-1990s, the U.S. Department of Defense began negotiations with the Japanese government to decrease the U.S. military's footprint in Okinawa by moving Futenma Air Station out of the crowded center of Ginowan City to a more rural area of the island (Henoko) and moving eight thousand Marines off-island. This agreement was signed in 2006 and reaffirmed in 2012, but implementation has met with stiff opposition both in Henoko, Okinawa, where the new base is to be built, and in Guam, where many of the Marines are slated to go. Activists have engaged in civil disobedience, such as chaining themselves to scaffolds being erected in the ocean where the new base is to be built near the shoreline. They have also held vigils, taken part in mass protests, and relied on solidarity from groups on the Japanese mainland and around the region.

In 2009 political developments in Japan appeared to turn in favor of activists in Okinawa. Yukio Hatoyama of the opposition Democratic Party of Japan became Prime Minister after promising in his campaign that the Futenma Air Station would be removed from Okinawa altogether and not just relocated to another part of the island. The United States, however, immediately pressured Hatoyama to keep the U.S. base in Okinawa. After a few tense months he publically capitulated, saying that Japan needed the Marines in Okinawa for reasons of "deterrence" and that he would go back on his campaign promise and allow the base to stay in Okinawa. Because of this action, Hatoyama was forced to resign. He later admitted that the Marines (which are by training an offensive strike force) did not serve as a deterrent and that he used deterrence only as a "pretext" (Satoko, 2011). He candidly admitted that U.S. pressure and bureaucratic obstruction from within his own government made it so that he could not, even as Prime Minister, get the base removed from Okinawa. At the end of December 2013, in a further illustration of politicians' difficulties in stopping bases, Okinawa governor Hirokazu Nakaima reneged on a 2010 campaign position that a replacement for Futenma should not be built in Okinawa, signing an agreement with the Japanese central government to allow construction to begin in Henoko. These experiences in Okinawa have only bolstered the belief of antimilitarization activists that engaging in a "politics of demand" with the state and trying to get "friendly" candidates elected to political office are ineffective strategies compared with direct-action tactics and mass protests.

VIEQUES, PUERTO RICO

Although Puerto Rico is not in the Pacific region, the situation in Vieques, Puerto Rico, is instructive for two reasons. First, it shares a similar militarized history to many of the islands in the Pacific. Second, its case is well known in Pacific activist circles because the island's citizens succeeded in kicking the U.S. military off their military-dominated, colonial island. Antimilitarization activists in Puerto Rico and Pacific islands have reciprocally shared strategies and tactics, and therefore it is difficult to examine antimilitary activism in the Pacific region without stepping out of the region for a moment to consider the case of Vieques.

The U.S. military acquired most of the island of Vieques during World War II by expropriating the eastern and western thirds of the island and forcing the approximately ten thousand inhabitants into the small central area. In subsequent decades the U.S. Navy used the island for aerial bombardment, shelling from warships, and practice invasions. During a period of heavy use in the 1980s the island was subjected to an average of 3,400 bombs dropped, 158 days of naval bombardment, 200 days of air-to-ground combat exercises, and 21 days of Marines practicing invasions each year (Aldrich & Connell, 1998). As a result, there has long been opposition to the Navy's use of the island. In the 1960s and 1970s, the fishing community was active protesting the military and would sail into the military area to interrupt exercises (McCaffrey, 2002). Protests continued throughout the 1980s and 1990s, but they expanded tremendously in 1999 after an errant bomb killed local Vieques resident David Sanes. After his death, the protest movement launched a variety of campaigns. In Vieques, activists have used protest tactics similar to those used in Hawai'i, Okinawa, and other militarized islands. Protesters occupied the bombing range and blockaded the gates between the civilian and military areas. These acts of civil disobedience blocked maneuvers in the range between mass arrests. Vieques also benefitted from a wide-ranging solidarity network in other parts of Puerto Rico and the world. In the year 2000, over 150,000 people took part in demonstrations in San Juan to call for an end to the bombing, and six people draped the flags of Puerto Rico and Vieques on the Statue of Liberty's crown to publicize the plight of Vieques.

The coalition of groups that came together to oppose the military use of Vieques was politically quite broad. While there were certainly avowed anti-imperialist and antimilitarist *independentistas* working in solidarity to end the militarization of Vieques, there were also a number of groups involved from decidedly nonradical backgrounds. Eventually health care workers, teachers, students, leaders and members of local Protestant and Catholic churches, the Puerto Rican procommonwealth party (PPD), and even Republican New York governor George Pataki ended up calling for the Navy to leave Vieques (McCaffrey, 2002). Under this intense barrage of local civil disobedience, solidarity actions, and political pressure, the Navy closed the bombing range in Vieques in 2003.

What is to be made of the fact that these politically broad, but geographically local, coalitions were formed against militarization in Vieques alongside an effective international solidarity network? On one hand, many activists in Vieques claim that the broad coalitions were absolutely essential to achieving their victory. While networks at the level of the island and the Puerto Rican archipelago were politically and socially broad, the protest movement also depended on a broad geographical support network from Puerto Rican constituencies in the United States as well as solidarity with anti-imperialist, antimilitarist, and peace groups from around the world. Particularly noteworthy were the connections people on Vieques started making with people from other places who opposed militarization in their home communities. Groups from Japan, South Korea, the Marshall Islands, and Hawai'i came to Vieques, while people from Vieques made visits to militarized islands in the Pacific.

Through the different networks and protest tactics, activists on Vieques were successful in redefining security on their island. Activists emphasized the island as a space for living and not a no-man's-land (gendered language intentional) where practices of destruction are acceptable. They managed to make visible not only the destruction and death caused by militarization but also the life of Vieques. At sites like Vieques, activists have shown that militarized islands are not only places of domination but also important sites from which imperial domination can be unraveled. With the closing of the testing range on Vieques, the large nearby Roosevelt Roads military base on the main island of Puerto Rico also closed.

Part 2: Imperial Reactions to Resistance

The Department of Defense is keenly aware that the structure of their base network can be affected by opposition in the locales in which they want to operate. Former defense secretary Donald Rumsfeld opined that "the presence and activities of our forces grate on local populations and have become an irritant for host governments." He claimed that "prudent U.S. relocations could reduce frictions with local populations, especially in Okinawa and South Korea" (Critchlow, 2005, p. 10). When deciding how to restructure the network of U.S. bases, the 2004 Defense Posture Review stated: "[W]e gave consideration to the irritants that our overseas military facilities can cause, particularly where such facilities are near host-nation population centers and valued land holdings. Wherever possible we looked to make posture changes that lessen the real and perceived burdens of such situations. Ultimately, these changes should help us to strengthen our alliances and improve our ability to interact with the host nation" (DOD, 2004, p. 7). In terms of frictions caused by military training, however, the military's reaction was not focused on how to minimize the environmental and social impacts of training, but rather to figure out how best to keep dissent from further interfering with their desired training activities. The military's view after losing the ability to train in Vieques is exemplified on the navy's website:

> Supporters of the military immediately criticized the Bush Administration's new plan [to end training on Vieques] on the grounds that it could lead to reduced readiness of U.S. naval forces and complicate the U.S. ability to maintain access

> to overseas training ranges in places such as Okinawa and South Korea. How might the Bush Administration's new plan affect the U.S. ability to maintain access to overseas training ranges where there is local opposition to U.S. operations, such as Okinawa or South Korea? Does the plan set a bad precedent for managing disputes over ranges, and will it encourage other local populations to step up their opposition to U.S. training activities? (http://www.history.navy.mil/library/online/vieques.htm)

After the loss of Vieques and training stoppages at Makua Valley and at Farallon de Medinilla in the Mariana Islands, the military began doing systematic studies aimed at keeping training areas and bases open. The National Defense Authorization Act for Fiscal Year 2003 required the DOD to make regular reports to keep training ranges functional. The two most salient terms that come up in these reports are *sustainability* and *encroachment*. In military training parlance, the "sustainability" of bombing and firing ranges refers to the military's ability to sustain training activities in the face of opposition. Meanwhile, *encroachment* is defined this way:

> The Deputy Undersecretary of Defense (Installations and Environment) stated that encroachment is any pressure, both internal and external to test and training ranges, that affects the ability to carry out live testing and training. Encroachment caused by external factors is an increasing threat to military readiness. DoD recognized that encroachment issues were important after local community concerns threatened to interrupt, interrupted, and/or terminated the testing and training activities at ranges on the island of Vieques in Puerto Rico, at Massachusetts Military Reservation, at Makua Valley Military Reservation in Hawai'i, and at Farallon de Medinilla in the Pacific Ocean. (DOD, 2002, p. 1)

Encroachment, therefore, is anything—physical, legislative, activist—that stands in the way of sustaining live-fire training. The language used here lays bare the military's view of the lands they occupy. In grand imperial fashion, the land does not belong to any of the former tenants of the land, the island governments on which the ranges are situated, or the populations who live adjacent to them. By referring to other potential land uses as "encroachment," the military erases the histories of seizure and occupation that brought the training ranges into their jurisdiction in the first place. (To extend the critique, it should be noted that many training ranges, when they were established, were supposed to be temporary or operational only until the end of a particular war or "emergency" of one kind or another.)

To help with the problem of encroachment on "their" ranges, the military hired a consulting firm, SRS Technologies, to develop a Sustainable Ranges Outreach Plan. A key finding of the study is that the military should change the name of their communication strategy. The report states, "DoD uses the word 'outreach' when dealing with local communities and writing draft policy; however, local communities and stakeholders consider outreach as one-directional communication. Using the term 'community involvement' would convey to the public a positive willingness by DoD to have two-way communication" (DOD, 2002, p. 11). Despite DOD attempts at "community involvement," people next to bases continue to oppose training activities in their surroundings because of the long list of deleterious effects. Training activities, and the spaces where the military conducts them, are therefore important nodes in military operations where resistance movements are often sparked. To paraphrase the old labor dictum that the "boss is the best organizer," the military's insistence that training *must* be carried out in proximity to forward bases has been the best organizing tool for activists resisting militarization. This resistance, in turn, continues to restrict the Pentagon's ability to build new bases and even maintain the ones they currently operate.

There are other issues around forward bases besides those dealing with training. While the military seems to have taken a somewhat oblivious position in dealing with opposition to its training activities, there has been recognition within the DOD that the overall impact of their bases in foreign countries is threatening the effective operation (and in some cases the very existence) of the bases. There is, therefore, a desire by the DOD to locate U.S. troops and bases, as Donald Rumsfeld put it in 2005, "Where they are wanted, welcomed, and needed" (Critchlow, 2005, p. 10). This attitude is echoed in more recent publications put out during the Obama Administration, such as the 2010 Quadrennial Defense Review, which notes that "America's defense posture should provide a stabilizing influence abroad and be welcomed by the host nation. Forward stationing and rotational deployment of U.S. forces are designed to contribute to regional security and will be enhanced, lessened, or reshaped as necessary to reassure allies and partners and strengthen deterrence" (DOD, 2010, p. 87).

Where are these places that welcome militarization? Many U.S. bases and training areas have been removed from strategic locations from the Philippines to Puerto Rico, and protests, political upheaval, and foreign court rulings currently threaten the status of bases in locations from Kyrgyzstan to Diego Garcia. Furthermore, the U.S. military is concerned that even in places where its bases are fairly secure, their freedom to operate could be hampered by restrictions on training and host nation sensitivities to the types of deployments made from, or through, their territories. Lincoln Bloomfield (2006), former U.S. assistant secretary of state for Political Military Affairs, put it this way:

> Senior DoD officials emphasized the "usability" of American forces stationed abroad, referring to political constraints that host countries might place on them in a crisis. . . . Governments take an appropriate interest in how their territory is used and accord special political significance to any scenario in which another country's forces launch combat operations directly from their territory. There is an implied complicity on the part of the host nation in the military objectives of the forces' mission. Host governments—democracies above all—can be expected to require prior consent. . . . Host countries that would impose nettlesome constraints on the out-of-country deployability of U.S. forces should not expect to be significant hubs in the new American defense posture. (pp. 56, 61)

In short, the military is reacting to constraints put on their operations by searching for base sites that not only give global coverage (see chapter 2) but also enable *operational unilateralism*. In contrast to political unilateralism, a doctrine under the George W. Bush administration of waging war without the political agreement of the United Nations or significant allies, operational unilateralism is the military's ability to strike quickly without needing consultation with anyone—even the government of the territory from which they are launching the strike. The 2004 Global Posture Review explained the concept in this way: "An important facet of our global posture is our system of legal arrangements with allies and partners. With some countries we will need new legal arrangements, and with others we may need to update existing arrangements. While mindful of sovereignty and country-specific concerns, legal arrangements that enable our global posture should maximize our ability to: Conduct training in host nations; Deploy U.S. forces wherever and whenever they are needed; and Support deployed forces around the world" (DOD, 2004, p. 15).

While most colonial powers throughout history have sought the unfettered ability to operate their militaries wherever they wanted, the current U.S. doctrine attempts to gain this ability while trying to appear to be operating within the principles of the Westphalian system (i.e., respecting the sovereignty of other recognized countries). While paying lip service to other countries' sovereignty, the United States argues that the speed at which force must be deployed nowadays necessitates operational unilateralism. In the military view of the world, threats do not just potentially emanate from everywhere but also arise at potentially any moment. Therefore, forward military units must be globally deployable and also able to deploy rapidly. Pentagon doctrine holds that in the contemporary security environment of rapid terrorist attacks and "ticking bombs," consultation with allies (not to mention the U.S. congress) is a passé, time-consuming nicety that does not fit in with the speed at which lethal military force needs to be deployed (Hannah, 2006).

While this quest for operational unilateralism arose concurrently with the Bush doctrine of political unilateralism, it is still very much in operation today. Although the 2010 Quadrennial Defense Review, done under the Obama administration, has extensive rhetoric that clearly tries to distance their administration from Bush-era policies surrounding the Iraq invasion, it does not mince words about maintaining the military's ability to act unilaterally. The report states, "America's Armed Forces will retain the ability to act unilaterally and decisively when appropriate, maintaining joint, all-domain military capabilities that can prevail across a wide range of contingencies" (DOD, 2010, p. 10). This continued quest for operational unilateralism has serious ramifications for both U.S. constitutional law and international law (see, for instance, C. Johnson, 2007), and it also affects the geography of the base network. As the above quotes suggest, the military is looking for base sites with prearranged permission to train and deploy without negotiation. The problem is that other governments are becoming more reluctant to grant such permissions. Why would an allied government want to host a forward base that, by the Pentagon's own admission, no longer exists to defend the country in which it is placed, but instead is a site for training exercises (that raise the ire of people living adjacent to it) and a site for the projection of force (that the allied government is not going to be consulted about)?

So where do you put bases in the Asia-Pacific region to enable global reach and operational unilateralism? In short: colonies. Carnes Lords (2006), editor of the Naval War College Press, put it this way:

> Very recent experience—notably, the Turkish denial of access to U.S. ground forces in the run-up to the invasion of Iraq in 2003, and the closing of the American air base at Karshi-Khanabad in Uzbekistan in 2005 after the United States criticized its government's repressive behavior—shows clearly enough that there will always be uncertainties in the conditions attaching to the use of American forces stationed or operating on allied or friendly territory. It is therefore essential to consider other alternatives. There are three such alternatives: basing in the continental United States (CONUS), in sovereign U.S. territories overseas, and at sea. An alternative that has not been discussed as much as it deserves is the use for military purposes of sovereign U.S. territory overseas. There are two prime candidates here, Hawaiʻi and Guam. (In essentially the same category is the small British-owned island of Diego Garcia in the Indian Ocean.) (p. 5)

The U.S. military, it seems, has found a solution for many of the problems it faces in building a global network of bases unfettered by the constraints of allied governments and people: overseas sites like Hawaiʻi, Diego Garcia, and Guam. The military's intensification of their use of U.S. overseas territories, however, comes with its own set of problems. First, there have been plenty of effective popular protests that have affected military activities in overseas territories like Puerto Rico (Vieques), Hawai'i (Kaho'olawe and Makua Valley), Guam, and the Northern Mariana Islands (Farallon de Medinilla). Furthermore, imposing bases on these islands comes with a painfully obvious political irony. The United States is using territories denied basic rights of freedom and self-determination to use military force that, ostensibly, is being used to promote these same values. Increasingly, these islands are becoming fallbacks where the United States is moving bases (and their associated bombing and training areas) that are not tolerated elsewhere in the world.

GUAM AND THE NORTHERN MARIANAS

In this section I focus on Guam and the Northern Mariana Islands because they are currently slated to experience a massive increase in militarization over the coming decade. Guam, an island of 209 square miles and an estimated 160,000 people, has been a colony for close to five hundred years (see map 2 in chapter 1). Visited by Magellan, the island was under Spanish rule from the 1500s until it was acquired, along with Puerto Rico and the Philippines, by the United States after the Spanish-American War (Rogers, 1994). During World War II the island was controlled by the Japanese until a successful American reinvasion in July of 1944. After the war, the U.S. military took over 55 percent of the island's land, and a third of the island is under military control today (Herman, 2008). The taking of land was not the only setback to the Chamorro people. Population transfer into the American colony since the end of World War II, together with the departure of Chamorro youths escaping the island's bleak economic opportunities (many, not coincidentally, join the U.S. military), has been responsible for making the Chamorro a minority in their own homeland (Bevacqua, 2010). The indigenous Chamorro people made up over 90 percent of the population of Guam until after World War II, but as of the year 2000 less than half of the population was listed as native (Herman, 2008).

In Guam, the Northern Marianas, and the other surrounding areas of Micronesia there has long been a mutually reinforcing relationship between military use and lack of sovereignty (Herman, 2008). The United States won the Micronesian islands in the western Pacific as prizes in wars: Guam from Spain, and most of the rest of Micronesia from Japan after World War II (including the quasi colonies of the Commonwealth of the Northern Mariana Islands, the Marshall Islands, the Federated States of Micronesia, and Palau). There are some differences between the political arrangements different areas of Micronesia have with the United States, but they share the fact that residents of these islands can travel to the United States and can serve in the U.S. armed forces, but they have no voting representatives in the U.S. government.

While economic colonialism has been less intensive in these islands than in some other parts of the globe, Guam has turned into a major U.S. military hub, and the rest of Micronesia has become a region plagued by the legacy of nuclear weapons testing (see chapter 3) and is currently an area of "strategic denial," where other militaries are denied access and the United States maintains an official monopoly on military force. The main reason why these areas have been denied full independence is their strategic value and the fact that they contain U.S. bases (Petersen, 1998). In turn, these islands have been the sites of the intensive military activities that are increasingly hard to conduct in places with political sovereignty.

This denial of rights to people in Micronesia, the erasure of their social histories, and the portrayal of their islands by military planners as "anchored aircraft carriers" lacking any worth beyond locations for power projection and weapons testing has been remarkably consistent from World War II to the present. As noted, Henry Kissinger famously remarked about the region in the wake of American nuclear weapons testing in the 1950s, "There are only 90,000 people out there. Who gives a damn?" (G. Johnson, 1980). Today, politicians and military commanders continue to discuss the region as if the region's inhabitants did not exist, or at least lack the full agency of other people (existing as "bare life"). Guam's political status as a UN recognized colony is rarely questioned (and of course, neither is the military's complicity in creating and maintaining that colonial status). Dick Cheney's former deputy assistant for national security affairs, Stephan Yates, summed up the position best when he said of the military's ability to use Guam, "When God gives you a gift, it's good to use it" (Weaver, 2010). Of course, Guam did not become a military colony because God gave it to the United States, but rather through a long process of concerted colonization in which many branches of the U.S. government participated over the past century (Bevacqua, 2010; Herman, 2008; Lutz, 2009; Rogers, 1994).

Still, U.S. military planners speak of Guam as a site of freedom: freedom to train and operate unilaterally in the Asia-Pacific region. Its status as an American colony is appreciated even though the language used to describe it is carefully worded to avoid the word "colony." It is usually just referred to as "sovereign U.S. territory" with no discussion of the problematic nature of how that has come to be, or how that status is maintained. As U.S. Navy lieutenant commander David Zielinski (2009) noted, "When asked in an interview about the advantages of Guam as a base, former Commanding Officer of Naval Base Guam, Captain Robert A. McNaught[,] reiterated the argument that the island's primary advantage [lay] in its political status. By being sovereign U.S. territory [*sic*], Captain McNaught indicated that U.S. forces could operate unconstrained from the political requirements of host countries, either in training or during actual conflicts" (p. 3). Other commentators also praise Guam as a site for docile cooperation with military objectives: "America needs a secure airfield from which it cannot be denied access; political area denial could allow China to push American forces out of the region before or during a crisis. Guam has the advantage of being American territory, reducing the political difficulty of building and operating assets there. Furthermore, Guam, with its pro-military population and 7.7 percent unemployment, is unlikely to offer local opposition to increased military infrastructure" (Erickson & Mikolay, 2006, p. 22). When asked in 2007 why the eight thousand Marines from Okinawa were going to be moved to Guam, U.S. Marine lieutenant general John Goodman said, "Why Guam? The answer is because I can't go to the Philippines. If our alliance with the Philippines would allow us to go there, I would move 8,000 Marines right now to Manila Bay" (quoted in Cole, 2007). In this comment is the "present absence" of what Guam is capable of deciding. The Philippines can say "no," but colonized Guam has no such option.

As of 2013, the planned increase in military operations for Guam is slightly diminished but still extensive. Guam is now slated to receive only four thousand Marines from Okinawa (and their dependents), while the remaining Marines are expected to rotate to Australia and Hawai'i. Guam is still expected to host a new wharf for an aircraft carrier, a center for a new Global Hawk UAV (unmanned aerial vehicle) program, a missile defense site, and numerous training areas (some requiring the acquisition of more land). The military also plans to use other islands (Tinian and Pagan) in the nearby Commonwealth of the Northern Marianas for bombing and training. Assistant secretary of the Navy B. J. Penn called the increased militarization of Guam the "largest project that the Department of Defense has ever attempted" (Natividad & Kirk, 2010, p. 1). In 2009 the military's Environmental Impact Statement (EIS) predicted that the island of Guam, which has a population of close to 160,000, would have over 79,000 additional residents by 2014 as a result of the buildup. While these numbers have shifted downward in subsequent years, the predicted consequences still include increased damage to the physical environment through greater pollution, more intensive military use of Guam's already stretched water supply system, and the intentional destruction of almost eighty acres of live coral reef in Apra Harbor. Social consequences range from overburdened local utilities, schools, and hospitals to increased traffic, sexual assaults, assaults, robberies, and car accidents. Even though the U.S. EPA gave the military's EIS its lowest possible rating and said that the plans "should not proceed as proposed," the military still intends to go ahead with most of its plans, but with lower numbers of Marines and a longer timetable for completion.

Despite the military's intention to move the buildup of Guam along at the

FIGURE 7. Protest on Guam. Photo by author.

fastest possible speed, and military planners' descriptions of Guam as an ideal location for operational unilateralism, there is resistance on Guam—particularly from the native Chamorro population (Aguon, 2005, 2006). Many residents claim that the sexual harassment, assault, noise, environmental contamination, and loss of access to traditional land that they have been experiencing on their militarized island are likely to worsen with military expansion. When early plans for the Guam buildup were discussed in 2006, there was not a lot of vocal opposition from residents of Guam, but a protest movement against the buildup surged into prominence during the EIS process in 2009.

As at other military sites, a particularly contentious issue has been training. On Guam the military has insisted that it needs to increase its already substantial footprint to conduct live-fire training for Marines. The military EIS calls for taking land in an area called Pagat on the northeast coast of Guam. The land contains many Chamorro historical sites, and resistance has come from community groups, the Guam legislature, and the local historic preservation office. Despite the fact that this desire for new land takings has galvanized opposition to the entire buildup, the military maintains that it is absolutely necessary. The Pacific Division director for the Marine Corps, Bryan H. Wood, is quoted as saying, "The most important thing for the Marine Corps is we do have to have individual firing ranges somewhere here on Guam in order to train the Marines. We simply can't do it anywhere else—it would ruin our operations here" (Matthews, 2010, p. A-3). The idea of training elsewhere, or changing the way training is done to have less impact, is not seriously discussed. Rather than being viewed as having some legitimacy, the local resistance ends up being treated as "encroachment." Regardless, activists on Guam have managed to "encroach" on the new firing range. In late 2011, in response to a lawsuit submitted by activists, the Navy announced they were delaying plans for putting in the firing range at Pagat until they could complete another multiyear environmental impact assessment of the project. But even though the plan for Pagat is stalled, as of 2014, the military is looking to expand training areas in the Northern Marianas on both Tinian and Pagan islands (Camacho, 2013).

To conclude this discussion of the local effects of militarization and colonialism I want to make a few explicit points. First, while faraway power centers may place bases in islands at the imperial margins to bolster a militarized notion of security, the daily operation of these bases and training areas has negative in-place effects that leave residents *less* safe and secure. Second, due to these negative environmental and social effects, resistance movements have arisen to reclaim security through political action aimed at demilitarizing landscapes and reclaiming sovereignty. Third, some of these actions have been successful and caused bases and training areas to close or move, or for military activities to be curtailed. Fourth, demonstrating how militarization and colonialism are *increasingly* mutually reinforcing, the U.S. military has responded to these pressures from social movements (and wary governments) by shifting bases to spaces with less organized civil-society resistance movements and with more blatantly colonial forms of governance. Fifth, this spatial "dance" regarding where bases are going to be located around the region—driven by the contest between social movements and antagonistic military planners—is still very much continuing.

This fifth point is demonstrated by the enormous fluidity of the situation in the western Pacific. As discussed in this chapter, military planners were initially quite confident that increasing the military footprint on Guam would be a simple matter. Due to resistance from residents of Guam, as well as from key U.S. senators and Japanese politicians concerned about its cost, it has proven to be anything but simple. As a further example of the region's political fluidity, one of the reasons why the U.S. military became so dependent on Guam in 2009 and 2010 was that other countries in the region such as Thailand, Singapore, the Philippines, and Australia initially refused to accept any of the military units being moved out of Okinawa. In 2011 and 2012, however, these governments changed tack and have agreed to a greater U.S. military presence on their soil.

Given the U.S. military's ability to rapidly shift their base posture around the region, activists have employed spatial strategies of their own in an effort to make one island's demilitarization success not just another island's burden. Activists have become more explicit that antimilitarization efforts cannot be aimed and performed with only the local scale in mind. To this end, there has been a greater focus on networks of affinity and solidarity that span the region and the globe. In chapter 6 I analyze the regional and global forms of antimilitarization and anticolonial activism as well as the ways in which this affinity-seeking power is arrayed against projects for militarized hegemony. Before that, however, it is necessary to delve into one more theme in order to present a full picture of the context in which this contest between local groups and distant hegemons is playing out. That theme is the complex and often paradoxical interactions among militarization, colonialism, and island environments, examined in the next chapter.

CHAPTER 5

Colonialism, Militarization, Tourism, and Environment as Nexus

As I aim to demonstrate in the previous chapters, militarized landscapes are filled with not only social and political issues, but environmental ones as well. Bombs, munitions, fuels, and solvents used by modern militaries spread chemical and radiological contamination. Combat, maneuvers, and training tear up landscapes. Furthermore, the construction of bases, barracks, airstrips, and port facilities leave structures few people would consider natural. Military activities clearly have negative environmental impacts, and these threats to residents' health and local environmental security have been major catalysts for the development of protest and resistance movements.

Describing the relationships involving militarization, colonialism, and the environment, however, is a much more complex exercise than merely telling a story about landscape *destruction*. It is also a story of (ongoing) landscape control and landscape *production* (Robbins, 2012). A suite of activities have gone on, and continue to go on, in these militarized islands, shaping their social and physical environments in intense and pervasive ways that cause the impacts of militarization and colonialism to be even deeper than they initially appear. Colonialism and militarization are responsible for producing not only the built landscapes of the island but also tourist and conservation-friendly landscapes deemed to be "natural." Through this discussion I aim to present a fuller picture of just how much the landscapes of these islands have been, and still are, rearranged to suit the needs of outsider interests, including the U.S. military.

To tell this story I examine what I refer to as the colonial/military/tourism/environment nexus. This nexus is a collection of intersecting and reinforcing discourses and social practices that reshape landscapes and political decision making on Pacific islands for the benefit of outsider interests. How, though, are these four themes connected? On militarized islands from O'ahu to Guam and from Puerto Rico to Okinawa the projects of tourism, militarization, continued colonialism, and environmental preservation are intrinsically linked. For instance, military personnel are key tourism markets on these islands (Gonzalez, 2013; Teaiwa, 2000). Tourist amenities are also viewed as necessary for attractive military base sites (Gillem, 2007). Former military areas like Vieques and the

Chagos Archipelago are turned into wildlife refuges so the military can avoid expensive cleanups and deny residents' return to taken lands (J. S. Davis, 2007a; S. Davis et al., 2007; Vine, 2009). The military touts its new "green" programs like "One Guam, Green Guam" to portray military expansion as not just environmentally benign, but environmentally *helpful*. This is not to say that tourism and environmental preservation are inherently colonial or militaristic activities, but rather that in these colonized islands they tend to be directed and operated in such a way as to assist and enable militarization and a tightening of colonial control over the islands' landscapes. To illustrate this process, I revisit some of the sites already discussed in the book—namely, Guam and the Marshall Islands.

Some militarized landscapes are obviously scarred with bomb craters, the detritus of live-fire training, and the structures that enable military operations. Other militarized places, though, have a very different look. Many heavily militarized areas have recently been praised by environmentalists, tourists, wildlife managers, and travel writers as "pristine" and "natural." This in no way means, however, that these landscapes have been treated well. Quite the opposite is usually the case. Instead, outsider labeling of these landscapes as "natural" has served as a mechanism for outside interests—from colonial administrators to foreign entrepreneurs and the military—to wrest and maintain control of the islands as well as to avoid the cleanup of chemical and radiological contamination.

The term *nature* has a number of definitions, but a broad working definition is that nature is usually conceptualized as a "realm of extra human objects and processes existing outside of society" (N. Smith, 1984, p. 2). As many scholars—particularly political ecologists—have noted, the labeling of any environment as "natural" is usually not a statement of fact about some kind of never-before-touched landscape as much as it is a rhetorical attempt to erase the social histories that produced the landscape (Braun, 2002; Robbins, 2012). In other words, places may be labeled as "natural" because no discernable impacts of human activity are *visible* in the landscape, but it is highly likely that the landscape is the result of both environmental and social processes. In the case of the militarized landscapes I examine in this book, many of the supposed "natural" landscapes in militarized areas are conceptualized as such only through a double erasure of social history. First, there is an erasure of the social life that existed in the place prior to its takeover by the military. Second, there is an erasure of the history of the military's use. This is nowhere more evident than in places like Bikini Atoll and Guam.

The landscape of Ritidian Point on Guam offers an interesting point of entry for a discussion of the colonial/military/tourism/environment nexus (J. S.

Davis, 2007b). Ritidian Point on the northern end of Guam was under U.S. Department of Defense control from World War II until the mid-1990s, when administration of the area was turned over to the U.S. Fish and Wildlife Service (FWS). When visitors enter the FWS visitors' center that opened in 2007 at Ritidian Point, they are greeted by displays representing the surrounding landscape. The displays are divided into representations of the four ecological zones that fall into FWS jurisdiction: marine habitat, beach strand, back strand, and limestone forest. Each ecological zone's display is separated into the dichotomy of "Life as it was" and "Today." The displays present a narrative of paradise lost. Their texts list many culprits: invasive species, overhunting, bulldozers, industrial development, garbage, commercial development, abandoned cars, overfishing, nets that entangle turtles, broken and dying coral, ocean pollution, and habitat destruction. Conspicuous by its absence is any mention of the military presence on Guam. Even though Ritidian Point was under the military's jurisdiction for decades, there is no mention of the military's impact on this place. Visitors to Ritidian Point must drive miles along a road bordered on each side by high fences, labeled at frequent intervals with large signs warning motorists that they are passing through Northwest Field, a U.S. Air Force installation; however, the visitor center's displays say nothing of this. Not only is the word *military* missing from the displays, so too are the words *colonialism* and *dispossession*. The native Chamorro families that originally owned this land are still on Guam, and they seek a return of this land, but this is also not mentioned in the narrative. Simply put, the landscape of contemporary Guam is represented as a paradise *lost* rather than a paradise *taken*. The descriptions of degradation have an air of inevitability. It is destruction that comes from nature's contact with "people"—that vaguely homogeneous species that seems incapable of not haphazardly despoiling "nature" because it is in human "nature" to do so. This landscape in the wildlife refuge at Ritidian is presented as a natural place under threat but also as one that has to some degree been protected compared with other areas of Guam. Of course, this "protection" has come as a result of the land being taken away from its inhabitants and managed by the U.S. military.

This process is in no way specific to Guam. As this description of conservation on Guam would suggest, the nexus of relationships between militaries, colonialism, tourists, and environments can be complex. To show the depth of this complexity, I continue the discussion of Bikini Atoll that I began in chapter 3. While in chapter 3 I detailed the incredible destruction and contamination of the atoll, in this chapter I examine the paradox that the atoll is now viewed as a landscape more worthy of environmental conservation and visits from wealthy tourists than cleanup and indigenous habitation.

Seeing the Imperial Paradise on Bikini Atoll

While there are many differences between how vacationing or visiting individuals see places and how government and military institutions see them, understanding how foreign visitors see militarized places like Bikini Atoll is very instructive for understanding the colonial/military/tourism/environment nexus. For one, many of the tourists are from the imperial centers and carry with them the beliefs and prejudices about places common in institutions like the military (as shown in chapter 3). Second, tourism is a major economic engine in American colonies and is often intimately linked with American military activities (Gonzalez, 2013; Teaiwa, 2000). More importantly, tourism is worth looking at because, by definition, it involves people traveling from their own places into someone else's. It is, then, a good window for looking at how individuals see places as "for them" even when they do not live there. This perspective is, after all, one of the roots of seeing like an empire.

Many researchers have shown that tourism, like militarization, produces "other-directed" landscapes that can sever the connection between local conceptualizations of place and the resulting fabric of the physical landscape and its associated social activities (Urry, 1990; DeOliver, 1996; Hoelscher, 1998; Oakes, 1997; Chang, 2000; Cheong & Miller, 2000; D'Arcus, 2000). As Tim Edensor (1998) puts it, "In a neo-colonial process, it is often imagined that it is the right of the wealthy contemporary tourist to travel the world in search of difference—parts of the world are colonized by tourists (with their enclaves and colonies) and their distinctive tourist infrastructures and technologies" (p. 22). From this perspective it would seem that the introduction of tourism on Bikini, like military colonialism in the past, would again deny Bikinians the ability to refashion Bikini Atoll according to their desires. Tourist conceptualizations of the site, however, are only one set of current imaginings. Many Bikinians still view the atoll as a potential homeland.

In 1996, the Bikinian government started operation of the tourist resort on Bikini Atoll. In 2008 they suspended the operation due to high costs and an unreliable local airline. Some commentators were critical of the endeavor; Teresia Teaiwa (2000) commented, "Needless to say, the transformation of 'a nuclear graveyard' into a tourist site that might generate revenues for the Bikinians seems both symbolically and materially bankrupt" (p. 109). The resort was successful in attracting tourists during its years of operation. The Bikinian government, which goes by the poly-local moniker of the Kili-Bikini-Ejit Council, is based on Majuro Atoll in the southern Marshall Islands and is composed of an elected council and mayor that represent Bikinians living on Kili Island and Ejit Island (which is located on Majuro Atoll). The government-run resort on

Bikini, however, was over four hundred miles from the population center on Majuro and, as one of its employees noted, was "modest on amenities and high on diving" (personal communication, 2002).

Scuba divers from around the world converged on Bikini Atoll to stay in the simple hotel, stroll the white sand beaches, and dive among the wrecked warships that lay on the bottom of Bikini's lagoon. The resort attracted high-dollar tourists who were qualified to do the deep and technical dives, many of which are over 55 meters (175 feet) deep and involve swimming into the wrecks. In addition, divers had to do a series of decompression stops underwater where they breathed a special blend of air (Nitrox) before surfacing. The price for a week was US$2,700, not including the substantial airfare to get to Bikini. Most tourists stayed on Bikini for one week and spent much of their time diving.

The ships on the bottom of the lagoon have a history almost as complex as the atoll. The most famous vessels are the battleship USS *Arkansas*, the aircraft carrier USS *Saratoga*, and the Japanese battleship HIJMS *Nagato*.[1] The ships were sunk during the atomic tests in 1946, after which they were largely ignored. In the 1970s they rated mention only as "numerous obstructions" on the charts of Bikini's lagoon (Pincas, 1975). In the 1980s, however, title to the ships was transferred to the Bikinians because they viewed the scrap metal as a possible source of income.

In 1989, the U.S. National Park Service's Submerged Cultural Resources Unit performed a study to assess the tourism potential of Bikini Atoll. The research resulted in a text that cataloged the ships in the lagoon, described their condition, and recommended a plan of action to turn the atoll into a national park (Delgado et al., 1991).[2] The authors of the park service document wrote in excited prose about the historical importance of the sunken ships and the potential for a military-themed, scuba-diving-oriented park.

While the national park status was never realized, the document fostered the idea that the sunken ships were a tourism resource. The Bikinians sent a delegation to Las Vegas to review offers from private corporations, including Club Med, for the development of tourism on Bikini (J. Davis, 1994). However, they opted to forgo corporate involvement in order to maintain financial and aesthetic control over the operation. While they initially formed a partnership with a small diving company based out of Majuro Atoll in the Marshall Islands, the Bikinians later owned and ran the entire business. This strategy was successful, and the Bikinian council distributed the annual profits to Bikinians in equal per-person shares given to the (often male) heads of household.[3]

While higher profits for the entire community were a key factor in the Bikinians' development strategy, other considerations also played a role. Initially, the Bikinians worried that an outside tourism company might allow divers to scavenge pieces of the ships and other artifacts from the age of nuclear testing, which are seen as cultural and economic resources. A lawyer working with the Bikinians commented:

> One of the most important issues was control. And the control was not so much the fiscal control . . . as the cultural and diving control. We looked at Truk [a wreck diving site in the Federated States of Micronesia that resulted from an American attack on the Japanese fleet in World War II] and we saw how these once pristine ships had been stripped of all their instrument panels and virtually anything that is movable. And we realized that if we didn't set this up the right way that was going to happen to Bikini. And we could sign a deal with the Acme Diving Company, but we wouldn't be out there, we wouldn't know what was going on. And clearly a diver slipping . . . $100 to a dive master would probably be able to take a tachometer off a plane, or a trinket off of something movable. And we felt that would be wrong. And we felt, OK if Bikini is going to open itself up to the public we wanted to keep it pristine. (personal communication, 2002)

While it may seem odd that there is a concern for maintaining the "pristineness" of a set of decaying ships that have been underwater over sixty years after being pulverized by nuclear weapons, divers were attracted to Bikini because the wrecks have been somewhat preserved in their postbombing condition. What may seem even more surprising is that the atoll itself is also currently spoken about as a "pristine" place. Take, for example, the following quotes. A manager of the resort stated, "It is a wilderness. This place hasn't been touched in forty years" (quoted in Kristof, 1997). Nicholas Kristof (1997) from the *New York Times* claimed, "The amazing thing about Bikini is how alive it is: a white sand island full of coconut palms swaying over a perfect turquoise sea, fish and sea turtles swimming languorously by the beach." Bill Curtsinger (1995) from *National Geographic* magazine wrote that "with fishermen absent for 50 years, Bikini's waters [have] returned to a rare, undisturbed condition" (p. 47). A tourist I met there in 2002 summed up her experience this way: "It is what you picture in your mind. . . . It's a remote, beautiful South Pacific island. Beautiful beaches. There's nothing to do. No television. No phones. It's what you want it to be. We all wonder why the Bikinians aren't here. It's such a beautiful place" (personal communication, 2002).

How is it that a former nuclear test site has come to be regarded as a pristine "natural" landscape? Furthermore, how is it that the activities of indigenous people in this landscape are now seen by some as threatening that nature? What I want to focus on in the following discussion of Bikini Atoll and its "pristineness" is not so much the irony of that designation as the political ramifications of this process when examining militarized and colonized landscapes across the region. In particular, the concepts of nature and contamination combine

FIGURE 8. Trash on Bikini. Photo by author.

in some unusual ways near American military facilities—ways that legitimize continued colonial control.

In the case of Bikini, while the native population has had scant lived experience on the atoll for the past six decades, the atoll has hosted tens of thousands of U.S. military personnel, scientists, and tourists. During the nuclear testing era the landscape was dominated by living quarters, bars, basketball courts, bunkers, docks, and trash. Today, not only is the landscape still moderately radioactive (mostly from Cesium 137 in the terrestrial food chain), but much of the vegetation on the two main islands of the atoll consists of the straight rows of coconut trees planted by the U.S. Department of Energy in the 1960s (figure 5 in chapter 3). Concrete bunkers and other structures remain scattered around the atoll, and one end of the main island serves as a dump where trash and abandoned vehicles have been left to decay. Given these conditions and the reasonably well known history of nuclear testing, it seems odd that the atoll is so widely regarded as "pristine nature."

There has been, however, an erasure of history on Bikini. Unlike in 1946, it is not the interaction of indigenous people in the natural environment being erased, but rather the modernist project of nuclear weapons testing. Like with the other erasures of history, there are, of course, political consequences. The erasure of nuclear testing from Bikini has happened in two complementary ways. First, as detailed by Teresia Teaiwa (2000), the prominence of the bikini bathing suit has enacted a discursive erasure of nuclear colonialism at Bikini. The dominant meaning of the word *bikini* in the Western world is the bathing suit rather than the atoll. Teaiwa argues that the bikini bathing suit "alienates the colonized referent of the commodity" (p. 99) by replacing the colonial history of nuclear testing, and the image of the disposed Bikinian, with the bikini-clad woman. The bikini bathing suit, she argues, through eroticizing female bodies and linking them to European and American mythologies of South Sea women, "has two colonized referents, and privileges (however minimally) one (generic South Sea noble savage) over the other (dispossessed Bikinians)" (Teaiwa, 2000, p. 99).

Complementing this discursive erasure of the colonial nuclear history on Bikini is the physical removal of many of the signs of nuclear testing from the landscape. Although the sunken ships at the bottom of the lagoon signal the site's history of nuclear weapons testing, these underwater relics are somewhat removed from the contexts of the testing program. Today, many of the visible signs of construction (and destruction) associated with the nuclear testing era on the land of Bikini Atoll have been cleaned and removed *from certain parts of the atoll*, especially on the main island, where most visitors stay. It is not that the artifacts of nuclear testing have simply eroded with time. Instead, there has been a concerted effort to remove these visible reminders. The visual appeal of Bikini's beach and reef landscapes forms the basis for the portrayal of the atoll as nature (see Bikini's beach in figure 4 in chapter 3). As for the issue of radioactive contamination, its invisibility renders it peripheral to the visually based conceptualization of the atoll. The atoll's radioactivity has affected the landscape, but the effects largely *support* the representation of the atoll as "natural." Dangerous radiation levels disallowed permanent habitation for almost fifty years. Even now, although Bikini's lagoon and most of the marine resources in it are generally regarded as safe, the terrestrial landscape is still considered too radioactive for long-term habitation (J. S. Davis, 2005a). There have been a few temporary residents (approximately twenty-five at a time) over the past decades who worked for the Department of Energy, the tourism operation, or a construction company hired by the Bikinians to maintain the infrastructure on the main island.

Seeing Nature on Bikini's Beaches

It may seem somewhat contradictory, if not downright weird, to be talking about a former nuclear test site as a pristine environment. Bikini, however, is not the only site of contamination to be thought of in this way. Locations near nuclear sites in the United States such as Savannah River, South Carolina; Hanford Reservation, Washington; and Oyster Creek, New Jersey, have been considered protected natural environments as well (Burger, 1998; Burger, Sanchez, Gibbons, & Gochfeld, 1997; Greenberg, 1997). As in the case of Bikini, the past labeling of these places as contaminated has restricted human activities and their accompanying impact on the environment.

Whether Bikini Atoll is "really" pristine or not is less my concern than the reality that many people who interact with the atoll conceptualize it as such. In my interviews with environmental scientists, tourists, tourism managers, Bikinian government officials, other Bikinians, and Republic of the Marshall Islands (RMI) government officials, the word *pristine* came up so often for describing Bikini that no discussion of the atoll's environment would be complete without analyzing the image of the place as a pristine wilderness (Shields, 1991; J. S. Davis, 2005b). Of the nine environmental scientists I interviewed on Bikini in 2002, five referred to the atoll directly as "pristine" and the other four described it as "untouched" or "unspoiled."

The lack of a large human habitation on Bikini Atoll has resulted in a very different oceanic and terrestrial environment than is found in the rest of the Marshall Islands and Micronesia. In particular, many visitors to Bikini Atoll note that the islands are relatively free of the trash and artifacts of modern consumer culture prevalent throughout the island Pacific. In stark contrast to the populated atolls of the Marshall Islands, the reefs on Bikini and other nearby nuclear-affected atolls are relatively free of refuse. Also, there has been almost no fishing pressure on the reefs. The visiting environmental scientists I interviewed made frequent comments that the reefs on Bikini were healthier and populated by a greater diversity of marine life than other areas in the Marshall Islands. Also, they mentioned that the members of the species found around the atoll (especially sharks) tended to be larger and more numerous than in other parts of Micronesia.

There is a desire among tourists and scientists working in the Marshall Islands to set up wildlife sanctuaries and conservation guidelines on all the nuclear-affected atolls across the northern Marshall Islands. For the most part, the local councils that govern these atolls are also interested in these conservation projects. The question then arises: Why here? What is it about these atolls that have been decimated by explosions and radiation that makes them candidates for conservation measures? While discussions about Bikini's pristine ecology are partially based on observations of biodiversity, fish size, coral health, shark populations, and bird behavior and endemism, the site's image as a pristine wilderness comes from more than just scientific information. Instead, most descriptions of Bikini's environment are based on a visual aesthetic environmentalism with deep philosophical roots in Western culture. Numerous theorists have discussed the primacy of the visual, termed *ocularcentrism*, that prevails in modern (or, as some would emphasize, postmodern) Western societies (Baudrillard, 1994; Rose, 2001; Evans & Hall, 1999; Barthes, 1981; Urry, 1990). As an example, the RMI government official in charge of tourism development said of Bikini: "When you go to Bikini you'll see. . . . The atoll, it's amazing. It's so pristine. Naturally. It's just turtles and birds and fish everywhere. I've only been in half of the 29 atolls in the Marshalls, but Bikini is definitely a very, very special place. . . . When you go there you realize that even before the testing it must have been a really, really special place, not just another atoll" (personal communication, 2002).

To say that most of the visitors to the atoll that I interviewed described Bikini as "beautiful" would be an understatement. Thirty-five of the thirty-six tourists I interviewed agreed that the label of "beautiful" should apply to Bikini. One of the marine scientists studying the atoll said: "It's just beautiful looking at the beach. It's not that common to see beautiful, sandy white beaches. Forget Majuro, or even Likiup or Ailingnae [other atolls in the Marshall Islands]—they don't have these long, beautiful, wide, white beaches. And then the contrast with the white and green and those blues in the lagoon—fantastic. I'm totally happy to just sit and watch the ocean even if I don't go dive" (personal communication, 2002). An official working for the Bikinian government also talked about the effects the visual beauty of the atoll can have on visitors: "I mean that was our best lobbying tool. We take these U.S. officials up there [Bikini], feed them steak and shrimp and let them walk on the beach and just say, 'This is what we gave up to you. Now you help us get back here.' Real simple. We didn't have to go up there and use, you know, do a lot of lobbying. It's just have them see the place. It's a very beautiful place" (personal communication, 2002). This emphasis on the visual beauty of Bikini is essential for constructing it as a wilderness area. It is also the reason why Bikini can be conceived as a pristine environment and a paradise, while at the same time being contaminated with (invisible) nuclear radiation.

The perceived beauty of landscapes, often more than scientific ecological findings, can be the basis of environmental preservation activities. Duncan and Duncan (2001) refer to this as "aesthetic environmentalism." Just as Duncan and Duncan found in their study in New York, many of the justifications brought up by scientists, tourists, and government officials for preservation at Bikini have to do with the preservation of pleasant "viewscapes" (both above and underwater). These conceptualizations of the island landscapes as worthy of environmental preservation, even when coming from scientists, arise not from a rational scientism, but from aesthetic concerns based on historical narratives of island paradises.

As is evident in the above quotes from scientists, tourists, and the media, it is not the whole visual landscape of Bikini that people focus on. Rather, their attention centers on the beaches. Beaches have become special sites of liminality that have great importance in tourism places. In Western culture "The Beach" has been constructed as a zone outside normal social conventions. It is a zone designated for play, for eroticism, and for gazing upon both landscapes and bodies. There is nothing natural about this, of course. Researchers have discussed how conceptions of beaches have changed historically (Doyle, 2005; Heaney, 2005; Shields, 1991; Taussig, 2000; Urry, 1990). Also, people from different cultural groups may view a beach as meaning very different things (as with any other place). But for the mostly American, Australian, and European visitors to Bikini, the beach is a zone for play and gazing.

The presence of beaches, however, is not the only reason Bikini is labeled a paradise. Bikini's beaches are Edenic because they are tropical and largely uninhabited. One tourist on Bikini exclaimed, "Oh my god, I'm the only one on this beach! I can see as far as I can see and I'm the only one" (personal communication, 2002). These beaches belong to a special category of landscape that is very significant in the Western imagination: the South Pacific island. This geographic label connects Bikini to other places. Bikini is thus assumed to share many of the characteristics of other "South Pacific islands." This does not necessarily mean that Bikini is believed to be like Rarotonga or New Caledonia (or for that matter Moruroa).[4] Rather, the term "South Pacific island" points not so much to a real geographical place as to an ideal setting that is a powerful Western cultural narrative. After all, Bikini's position 11 degrees north of the equator does little to dampen its appeal as a South Pacific island.

The Myths of Paradise

As discussed in chapter 3, this myth of the "deserted" South Pacific island is not merely of use to tourists and tourism operators. It is also an imperial construction that was used by the U.S. military to legitimize nuclear testing. The U.S. military may have used (and still uses) this rhetorical construct, but they did not invent it in 1946. Tourists also did not just find this myth. Instead, the place-myth of the deserted South Pacific island is an old and durable manifestation of the colonial/military/tourism/environment nexus that is useful for tourists, colonial administrators, environmental conservationists, and militaries alike.

This place-myth stretches far back into history and is widely disseminated.

Many scholars have discussed how the South Pacific narrative formed in European imaginations through imperial adventures and their associated literature, art, philosophy, film, and advertisements dating from the early moments of European awareness that the Pacific even existed (Dening, 1996; Desmond, 1999; Howe, 2000; Jolly, 1997; Lutz & Collins, 1993; B. Smith, 1960, 1992; Wilson, 2000). This imagining of the South Pacific as a paradise dates from early descriptions of Tahiti by British captain James Cook and other colonizing explorers, but it is still very much repeated to this day. In these representations the South Pacific island is portrayed as not just a geographical antipode to Europe, but its cultural antipode as well. A special kind of Orientalism has been applied to the Pacific. Rather than it being the space of the Asian "other" that serves as a threatening antithesis of the European (Said, 1979), the South Pacific islands have been imagined as a space of a more natural, primitive, pliable, and erotic other in a landscape often dubbed an "Eden."

Eden, as a concept about a supposed origin, paradise, or utopia, dates back in Western culture, some argue, to as long ago as 7000 B.C. (Grove, 1995). Over time, a remarkably stable set of attributes have been used to define what Eden is. Namely, Eden is a place where food supplies are bountiful, toil is unnecessary, and people, if they are there at all, are few in number. An Eden connotes wildernesses: a place where the impacts and actions of humans are sublimated by the powers of nonhuman forces, or "nature." While the definition of Eden has been rather stable, the geography of Eden—where it can be found—has changed dramatically over time. As David Arnold (1996), K. R. Howe (2000), Greg Dening (1996), and others have convincingly argued, there is a history to the way tropical islands have been constructed as Edens. While most scholars recognize the widespread application of Edenic narratives to tropical islands in the 1700s, especially in the Pacific, most argue that this was not the origin of discourses about Eden. Rather, this time period is marked by a shift in the location of Eden to the antipodes of Europe. There is nothing necessarily "natural" about the fact that this floating conceptualization of a place known as Eden, first applied to the area of present-day central Iraq nine thousand years ago, has now landed on islands in the tropical Pacific. Instead, there has been a merging together of the imagined geography of Eden with European experiences at physical sites on islands in the tropics.

These European visions of Pacific Edens, and the supposed "naturalness" of the people who inhabit them, are portrayed in a combination of negative and positive ways. The supposed primitiveness of the Pacific is not uniform but instead split into an uneasy dichotomy. Bernard Smith (1960, 1992) demonstrates through his analysis of European representations of the Pacific that there have been changes in the form that the naturalness of the Pacific takes both across space and through time. According to Smith, the representations fall into two forms of primitivism: a "soft primitivism" that extols the inviting fruitfulness of the landscapes and the virtuousness of premodern inhabitants as "in nature" (the noble savage trope) and a "hard primitivism" that portrays landscapes as harsh, diseased, and impenetrable and the inhabitants as fierce and uncivilized (the cannibal trope). These historical (and contemporary) representations of the landscapes and peoples of the Pacific as either "hard" or "soft" are often heavily gendered as well (Desmond, 1999; Dowler, Carubia, & Szcygiel, 2005; Jolly, 1997; Lutz & Collins, 1993; MacCormack & Strathern, 1980; Teaiwa, 2000).

Spatially, Europeans tended to mark Eastern Polynesia (in the eastern Pacific) with the soft primitivism label and Melanesia, Aotearoa/New Zealand, and Australia (in the southwestern Pacific) with the hard primitivism label. While there are a lot of exceptions to this generalization, much of it centers on European racial distinctions between lighter-skinned Polynesians and darker-skinned Melanesians. Bernard Smith (1960) also points out that there have been shifts in the dominant representations of the Pacific through time. Smith's work, which focuses largely on the age of early European exploration (late 1700s to the mid-1800s), demonstrates that the type of primitivism that dominates European representations changes based on events (such as the killing of Captain Cook in Hawai'i) and on the political and cultural climates in Europe.

It is clear that these early representations of the Pacific were applied unevenly in both time and space. However, Smith and others are struck by how these two types of primitivism are often applied to the same place at one point in time (Dening, 1996; Howe, 2000; Jolly, 1997; Lutz & Collins, 1993). This creates an uneasy tension in the representations, but at the same time it reinforces the overall impression of "naturalness" and "primitiveness" by adding elements of unpredictability, uncontrollability, and irrationality.

While much of Smith's work focuses more on historic representations of the Pacific, other scholars have shown that labeling the Pacific as a "natural" place (whether in its "hard" or "soft" form) is still a powerful discursive force. The image of the natural South Pacific has been perpetuated and reinforced through time through the writings of Rousseau, the paintings of Gauguin, plays such as *South Pacific* (which was popular enough to have a revival on Broadway until 2010), and television shows like *Gilligan's Island*. One only had to have watched the television program *Survivor* (whether set in Palau, Vanuatu, the Cook Islands, or the Marquesas) or view the exotic/erotic imagery used to woo tourist dollars to Hawai'i to see that this place-image is very much still in force.

How, though, does this image of naturalness get applied to ex–nuclear test sites and military outposts? First, a lacuna in the work of many of the people looking at early representations of the Pacific needs to be addressed: Micronesia. Bernard Smith (1960) makes brief mention of a European journal about Palau (p. 97), but there is not much of an effort to fit Micronesia into the generalized dichotomy of European representations of Polynesian-soft primitivism and Melanesian-hard primitivism. One notable exception to this oversight is the work of Lutz and Collins (1993), who show through their analysis of *National Geographic* articles that more recent portrayals of Micronesia have tended to borrow the trope of soft primitivism usually aimed at Polynesia. Lutz and Collins emphasize that *National Geographic* represents Micronesia as "out of historical time" and influenced by "the innocence of Eden" (p. 138).

As Lutz and Collins demonstrate, there has been a change through time in how *National Geographic* portrays Micronesia. In particular, the group of islands has been more frequently portrayed as a "paradise lost," a childlike place that is "growing up" and becoming developed and modern. The magazine's portrayals particularly emphasize the presence of refuse in the landscape as symbolizing a fall from an Edenic state of nature. This refuse in the Pacific landscape, especially on beaches, destabilizes the visual base of the social/natural dualism that, according to theorists such as Bruno Latour (1993), still resides in the modern psyche. Lutz and Collins (1993) analyze a 1986 photo of a polluted beach on Ebeye, on Kwajalein Atoll in the Marshall Islands, that has the caption, "pollution in paradise, junk overwhelms a beach." They contend,

> [B]eaches are the essence of the Pacific for many Westerners, as travel posters attest; the beach should be a scene of pleasure, not of work or unpleasant sights. If the Pacific is a paradise, as the caption and countless other cultural images tell us, then our despoiling of it is sacrilege here, merely commonplace elsewhere. Moreover, the 1986 lagoon suggests something not just about the Pacific but about the potential end to the dualism of the civilized and the natural human. The tragedy suggested by the picture and its caption is the end of our ability to define ourselves by way of this long-standing dualism. (p. 140)

The contemporary beach at Bikini Atoll, in contrast, reaffirms the dualism. Through its correlation, *visually*, with established cultural representations of what the natural Pacific ought to be, the empty and clean Bikinian beach confirms the nature/society dualism. Bikini is extolled as an Eden. It serves as a visual counterpoint not just to the profane spaces of modernity in urban Europe or the United States, where people and trash are an expected part of the landscape, but also to the fallen nature of other Micronesian islands. Even though knowledge of the nuclear history and radiation risk gives some a sense of unease, visitors' overwhelming response to the atoll is that it is a pristine wilderness that needs to be preserved. Several visitors referred to Majuro Atoll, the capital of the

Marshall Islands with over twenty thousand inhabitants, as an example of what might happen to the "natural" Bikini if it were not protected (J. S. Davis, 2005b). One of the environmental scientists studying Bikini used Majuro as a cautionary example: "You can't have a reserve and at the same time have 500 people living on it. To keep this pristine place, for naturalistic and biodiversity reasons, and for touristic reasons, if you have people living here [it must be] in a considerate way. Not as they are doing in Majuro. Majuro is doomed" (personal communication, 2002).

Bikini as Eden, Part 2: The Bountiful (but Boring?) Garden

Western visions of a Bikinian Eden do have an impact on how the landscape of Bikini is managed. The atoll, however, is politically controlled by an elected local council, and within the Bikinian community there are very different conceptualizations of what Bikini is and what it ought to be. Even though community conceptualizations of the atoll are by no means uniform, they do counteract and resist the dispossessing rhetoric that spins out of the colonial/military/tourism/environment nexus. Intriguingly, Bikinian representations of the atoll, like those of visitors, share the same recurring portrayal of Bikini as an Eden. However, *the kinds of human activities that are imagined to be appropriate in an Eden differ dramatically between the two groups.* These different versions of Bikini as Eden inform quite different strategies for the current and future use of Bikini's resources.

Narratives about Eden are, in the end, narratives of loss. In Western culture the Eden myth represents an imagined place of origin (Merchant, 2004). As I discussed, the islands of the Pacific region are seen as places where people are not alienated from nature and the necessities of life are supplied without labor and deprivation. In Western culture, Eden is far away historically, but simulacra of it are created in the mythologized accounts of "South Sea islands" and in modern tourism landscapes. To the displaced Bikinians, however, paradise was lost quite recently.

Today, the Bikinian community remains exiled throughout the Marshall Islands, most on Kili Island. Very few Bikinians remain who have a living memory of life on the atoll. An exception is the approximately one hundred Bikinians who lived on the atoll for a few years in the 1970s. After their subsequent removal, this group did not want to return to Kili Island and instead formed the Bikinian community on Ejit Island on Majuro Atoll.

Like many of the visitors to the atoll, many of the Bikinians I spoke with also referred to Bikini as a paradise or Eden. Many used biblical metaphors and emphasized the gardenlike aspects of Bikini and the availability of edible plants and animals. In this respect it is not just the land of the atoll that is paradise but also the bountiful lagoon environment. The lagoon environment on Bikini is compared with the lack of one on their place of exile (Kili Island) and the overused and polluted lagoon environment of Majuro. One Bikinian man said, "We take the meaning [of paradise] from the bible, like Adam and Eve. . . . It is a paradise, a place where you have everything you need. It is a place God puts you where all is within your reach. If you want fish, you go get one. Lobster, you walk out on the reef and get some, or crabs, or birds" (personal communication, 2001). The Edenic qualities of Bikini lie in the atoll not as a viewable landscape, but as a place where resources can be accessed. While this portrayal of the atoll as an abundant paradise was common, it did not always translate into a desire for a permanent return.

Currently there is no timetable for opening Bikini Atoll to long-term habitation. Estimates on when it will be safe for repatriation range from today to never. Since many Bikinians were exposed to high levels of radiation in the 1970s, the Bikinian local council is reluctant to allow anyone to move back while there is still uncertainty about the contamination. But what would happen if Bikini were declared safe tomorrow?

It is clear that the Bikinians would not return en masse and abandon Kili and Ejit Islands. Most of my interviewees believed it is more likely that some families would move back and that many others would visit or live there part-time. Some Bikinians already follow a path of circular migration between Kili, Majuro Atoll, and the United States. It is conceivable that Bikini Atoll would become another site in that circuit. This is not to downplay the importance of Bikini. While it may become only one place in which Bikinians live, it would be a highly significant place. Some of my interviewees have even suggested that the atoll may become a site of heritage tourism for Bikinians living elsewhere.

While not all Bikinians will become permanent residents if their atoll is declared safe, there is no doubt that some people will. Some Bikinians are more or less likely to return based on conceptualizations of radiation safety, but that is only one of the issues affecting repatriation decisions. Other factors include age, desire for the modern "city life" of Majuro, and landownership rights on Bikini. Those who are old enough to remember life on Bikini are the most adamant about returning. In sharp contrast, younger members of the community are unenthusiastic about moving to Bikini. One younger Bikinian woman living on Majuro said,

> There are people that just want to move back and then there are those people that say, "Why don't we just sell Bikini? What's the point?" . . . The older people

> though, "Oh, I wish I could spend my last years there." The younger people, no. I don't even think they have even been thinking about it like, "Someday I want to move back to Bikini." No. A lot of young girls that I talk to are like, "I just want to visit Bikini." "I want to see Bikini." But they don't say, "I want to live there." (personal communication, 2002)

To many younger Bikinians, the atoll is not just radioactive, it is boring. To them, it is an outer island that lacks the attractions of Majuro. These differences in attitude are due not just to who was alive in 1946, but to the generation gap caused by the rapid pace of modernization in the Marshall Islands. Stores, movie theaters, sporting events, cable television, and medical care on the capital atoll are draws to the younger generations of Bikinians. One young male Bikinian employee who worked on Bikini said, "I think Majuro is better than here. This [is an] outer island. On Majuro [there are] movies, friends, cars. [We can] go cruising" (personal communication, 2002). Another Bikinian male concurred: "I hear some younger people they talk about [Bikini being] too far, but they don't mention the radiation. They talk about too far, they don't have TV. You know, they think it is like an outer island. They like to go to mainland, Honolulu, stay in Majuro, use a lot of stores, cars, yes. Things to do, movies . . . Yes. And this generation now on Kili, I believe they don't know how to make copra. It is hard for them" (personal communication, 2002).

This generation gap is particularly illuminated by comments that if repatriation to Bikini is allowed, many older Bikinians would return and leave the younger members of their families behind on Ejit Island, Majuro, and Kili. One woman on Ejit said, "Well we feel like the older people could go back to Bikini but the younger ones they stay here and go to school for a better future. But we [will] move back to the island because there [are] a lot of trees: breadfruit, coconut . . . What we are going to miss [by leaving Ejit] is playing with the children, and that the doctor is near and the schools and everything" (personal communication, 2002).

Another major factor over who might return to Bikini is landownership. While all Bikinians have the right to *use* land on Bikini, the *ownership* of land, which follows a semimatrilineal system, is quite uneven and concentrated in the hands of heads of lineage known as "alabs" (Kiste, 1974). In the 1970s the main determinant of who returned to Bikini and who did not had to do with landownership. A Bikinian government official describes the motivation for one man to return to Bikini in the 1970s:

> He had huge tracts of land up there. Big tracts of land. And here on Kili he's just like everybody else and that's why he talks about land to a Marshallese is their

> form of gold. If you got a lot of land you are a very important person. You go down to Kili and everybody's got the same little chunk of land for their house. Suddenly you're just like everybody else and you feel like I should be getting a lot more because I'm a land owner and here's this Joe Blow guy over here who's maybe half a Bikinian or something, and not from his mother's side, where he's getting the same thing I am. You got a lot of resentment like that. But all the land lines on Bikini, everybody knows where they are. Everybody knows whose land it is. That never goes away. (personal communication, 2002)

The families that have ownership over large amounts of land on Bikini, and returned there in the 1970s, are the families that founded the community on Ejit instead of returning to Kili after their removal from Bikini. This group would seem to be the most likely to lead an eventual return to Bikini because of landownership and because, for many of them, their lived experiences on Bikini date from the 1970s and not the 1940s. There is, though, still a great amount of uncertainty about who would go back. One Bikinian council member summed it up well when he said,

> For now I'm not really sure which community [Ejit or Kili] will be most likely to move back. Because right now our elders have been [dying] right now. Almost all are young age now so I don't know if their mind is, you know, like their elders. . . . And another thing, our elders really didn't care about the radiation level on Bikini. Their mind was only to get back to the land. They don't care how high the radiation level. . . . Because they don't have any knowledge on radiation, but for our younger generation now that we've been understanding more about radiation so maybe it will make us scared to go back to Bikini unless we know that it is really 100% safe for us to live. (personal communication, 2002)

Even though there is uncertainty about who may move back to Bikini, there is a consensus within the community that Bikini is a paradise of *usable* natural resources with intense cultural significance. The differences in opinion are based on whether living in that kind of place is desirable. Since most community members have no direct experience with the atoll, and there is doubt about the safety of returning soon, some Bikinian government officials feel that the future for Bikini lies not in a return to subsistence living, but in using Bikini as a means to generate income through tourism and the associated preservation of the atoll's resources. As one official said, "We are planning to, if necessary, looking into it, establishing what we call the marine sanctuary. Because, you know, Bikini is one of the [atolls] known [for] the very, very, large sharks. There was a TV channel called Discovery that came to Bikini and they discovered that there is a pass full of sharks. I think people might be interested in this. Also we have a lot of turtles, seabirds, and we are pretty sure that it might be good for a marine sanctuary or something like that" (personal communication, 2002).

The Colonial/Military/Tourism/Environment Nexus, Resistance, and Versions of Eden

There are potential conflicts looming for Bikini Atoll. When Bikini is determined to be safe for repatriation, not all Bikinians will return, but many will. The people on the neighboring nuclear-affected atolls of Enewetak and Rongelap have already begun to return. What happens to the environmental imaginings of Bikini if a large number of people come back to the atoll and see it as a home with usable resources? What happens in regard to demands that the military do a full cleanup? Seeing Bikini as a homeland is in many ways at odds with the other conceptualizations of the atoll as "nature," in that designating a place as nature, according to the Western binary of the natural and the social, marginalizes the people in these places and discourages many social activities within them. Ecological parks and marine sanctuaries are not places where people live and work as much as they are places that are set aside for outsider-directed activities. In this way, spaces of environmental conservation can be seen as marginalized in much the same way as colonized places, vacation sites, and military areas (Cosgrove, 1998; Kirsch, 1997; Shields, 1991; Turner & Ash, 1976). This connection between preservation, tourism, and colonialism has been noted outside the Pacific region as well. Rod Neumann (1998), in his study of the establishment of a Tanzanian national park, mentions, "While the possibility of economic gains through tourism helped to motivate the state's efforts to protect and control natural resources, national parks are a unique form of resource management. They served as powerful symbols of a European-based vision of what Africa should be" (p. 123). Neumann's comments about the power of European imaginings of "what Africa should be" are similar to those made by K. R. Howe (2000) about tourism and conservation spaces in the Pacific: "They are Western cultural spaces, not the cultural spaces of the Other to whom they ostensibly belong. Pacific island tourism remains a colonialist activity, not just in social and economic terms, but in its intellectual/imagining process, even in these so-called postcolonial times" (p. 30). Just as Neumann contends that Western visions affect the reproduction of African places, there are effects on what Bikini will become not just because of scientific information, but because scientists and other visitors have been applying the narrative of pristine wilderness to the atoll. These aesthetic visions affect what Bikini "should be." Furthermore, this process is very much in operation at other military and colonial sites around the world.

So what happens when people move back to the atoll and have a desire to live there in ways that transgress its designation as pristine "nature"? Many tourists made comments about "shanties," garbage, and the danger that may come with having a native population around the resort. I asked visitors, both tourists and environmental scientists, what they thought Bikini would be like if five hundred Bikinians (one-seventh of the current Bikinian population) returned to the atoll. Most stated that they did not mind if Bikinians came back to the atoll as long as they lived in the environment in the "correct" way. Some tourists welcomed the chance to visit the atoll, do some diving, and also have a cultural tourism experience with "primitive" people. One male tourist said, "There could be a distraction if there were more people on the island. The other thing is that there are a bunch of islands around there. So maybe they might not come back to Bikini itself but one of the other islands that are already out there. Then you could go visit them and do the village thing" (personal communication, 2002). An American employee of the resort stated, "I'm not being judgmental. If that's the way they live, then that's the way they live. It just happens to be different than me. I don't care, but when you start talking about tourism I know what is acceptable and what will attract tourists and I know what is unacceptable and won't attract tourists. . . . The reality is if you've got a place with a lot of refuse around and there's motor vehicles, and the kids are allowed to play unattended and run back and forth across the street it's not going to attract the tourists" (personal communication, 2002). So in the tourist imagination a natural island can have native people, but it is not expected to have *modern people* (particularly ones viewed as untidy).

This sentiment was echoed in regard to the atoll's environment as well. The visiting environmental scientists, as well as employees at the resort, are wary of what may happen to Bikini's ecology if Bikinians return and do not live in certain prescribed ways. Their responses demonstrate a range of opinions about repatriation from it being a certain disaster for the atoll's ecology to it being reconcilable with environmental protection if "planned correctly." This wariness about the environmental effects of repatriation is generally associated with resource use by the Bikinians for subsistence, but some people also voiced concern about waste management and the potential for the Bikinians to engage in commercial fishing. Again, when discussing the potential impacts of a permanent community, many individuals used the heavily fished, polluted, and crowded Majuro as a comparison. One employee at the resort, regarding the idea of a large influx of Bikinians to the atoll, said, "The environmental impact, it would be as such that it would have massive amounts of decrease in fish, you would have massive concentrations of bird lossage. Unless they had some way of enforcing environmental rules and regulations this place would just be like Majuro very quickly" (personal communication, 2002).

Bikinians who see the atoll as a homeland with plentiful *usable* resources would likely resist continued restrictions over fishing and hunting. The visitor to the atoll, however, has the perspective of Bikini as a pristine wilderness and believes that the imaginings of the atoll as a homeland have to be brought into line with the "pristine wilderness" place-image, not vice versa. One marine biologist, displaying a neo-Malthusian logic, went as far as to suggest that it would be best for the "pristine nature" of Bikini to limit the number of Bikinians that could return:

> The pressure on the reef would be fairly intense and that would be a real pity, because this is probably one of the few places in the world where there isn't pressure on the marine resources. That's a pretty special thing to have a pristine reef. So it would be nice to be able to protect that. I think it would be good to have a few people back on the isle because there's been a population here, and it would be nice to have some sort of balance. It would probably be difficult to sustain 500 people I think. Maybe 200 might be a more appropriate limit. (personal communication, 2002)

It is helpful at this point to take a step back and remember that this is a former nuclear test site that people are talking about. They are enumerating the potential negative impacts of five hundred people engaging in subsistence fishing and hunting on an atoll that has been utterly laid to waste by twenty-three nuclear weapons and the associated activities of tens of thousands of military and Department of Energy personnel. In the debate over the preservation of the atoll, it is easy to overlook the fact that Bikini bears the scars of one of the most destructive modernist projects in the history of the world. Three islands were vaporized, and it is still considered dangerous to spend more than a few hours on the islands in the northern part of the atoll because of high background radiation. A crater a mile wide runs through the atoll reef. The vegetation on the islands on the far side of the atoll was annihilated by nuclear fire. Not to mention that Bikini and Eneu Islands have gone from forests of coconut trees and pandanus to nothing but scrub brush, and now to neatly planted rows of Cesium-137-tainted coconut trees.

I am not recounting this nuclear history to say that individuals who profess the pristine wilderness place-image are consciously guilty of deception, but rather to show the power of the representations constructed according to the logics of the colonial/military/tourism/environment nexus. At its foundation, what underpins the nexus is the paternalistic belief that the colonizer knows what is best for the place, even when the history of the place demonstrates, in the extreme, that this is a complete fallacy. In this case, the Edenic place-myth is so strong that proposing limits to the numbers and activities of a local population makes sense even when the Eden was created by nuclear weapons, displacement, and dispossession. If, however, Bikini is instead viewed as a site that has been a playground for U.S. military destruction, it sounds incredibly callous to suggest that foreign scientists should be making recommendations restricting how many people can fish in the lagoon so that the lagoon can be preserved as a unique specimen of biodiversity. I do not mean to attack the scientists themselves or to belittle the idea of environmental conservation. Rather, I caution against the negative political consequences of attaching the Eden place-myth to sites of colonial and military control because it shifts the scale at which people designate ownership of the resources away from local inhabitants.

I also note that this phenomenon of turning contaminated bombing sites into nature preserves is not specific to Bikini Atoll. These Edenic place-myths can have very direct practical consequences for people living next to active and recently closed military areas. As the earlier discussion of Guam demonstrates—and as is shown in research at contaminated sites including Vieques, Colorado, and South Carolina—the labeling of contaminated landscapes as pristine wildernesses in need of preservation is a trend seen in many places with military contamination (S. Davis et al., 2007; Havlick, 2007; Kirsch, 2007; Krupar, 2007). One important effect of this labeling on the future redevelopment of these places is that it usually keeps a site from being returned to its former owners. Claimants who had their landownership or use rights expropriated by the military have a difficult time reclaiming those rights because the property's designation as a wilderness often means the site remains under federal control. Furthermore, turning contaminated military areas into nature preserves tends to preserve more than just "nature": it also serves to *preserve the contamination*. For example, in places subject to CERCLA[5] (aka "Superfund") legislation, which includes U.S. colonial jurisdictions such as Guam, Puerto Rico, and the Marshall Islands (but importantly not U.S. military properties in Okinawa, South Korea, or the Philippines),[6] the level of cleanup required is based on future land use. If the future land use is deemed to be a wildlife refuge rather than a place of human habitation, the military can save tremendous amounts of money by cleaning contamination to a much lower standard (S. Davis et al., 2007).

Purification, Politics, and the Scales of Eden

Places like Bikini Atoll, when represented as a pristine wilderness, become sites in a global imperialist system of place imagining. Roderick Neumann (2003), drawing on the work of Denis Cosgrove, Raymond Williams, and others, claims that the landscape aesthetic in Western (particularly British) society has resulted in "the creation, materially and symbolically, of two distinct landscapes: one of production ruled by rationality and profit and one of consumption where recreation and contemplation prevail" (p. 241). The extensive literature on searches for Eden bears this out. A sacred, natural Eden is imaginable only in opposition to the profane social spaces of the modern subject that are seen as intrinsically divorced from nature. These supposedly "natural" landscapes like Bikini fit into a global system of place imagining that divides the world into civilized social spaces and natural Edens: a space for modern living, and a premodern "pleasure periphery" for tourism and ecology. In the case of tropical Bikini Atoll, the forces of modernity have created a visually appealing wilderness that places it in the latter category, with real implications for the future of the atoll. An environmental scientist said this about what she wanted Bikini to be in ten years: "[I want it to be] the same. . . . The only change that I would like to see, because I'm a marine biologist, I would like to have people interested in seeing the coral reefs. They're so special and so unique in the middle of the Pacific. . . . In terms of the structures around, nothing should be added. Nothing [should be] changed, it should stay the way it is" (personal communication, 2002).

This person is not alone in hoping that Bikini stays the way it is today. The sentiment is shared by many visiting scientists, tourists, resort employees, and some members of the Bikinian community. The problem, of course, is that keeping Bikini "the way it is" means maintaining its status quo as a place from which the Bikinians are still exiled. I do not mean to imply that people consciously oppose the return of the Bikinians so that the atoll can continue to be used as a tourism operation and an ecological park. The fact is, however, that a fair number do. All of the resort workers I interviewed expressed profound reservations about repatriation. Eight of the nine environmental scientists I interviewed believed that repatriation would threaten the ecology of the atoll. And only three of the thirty-six tourists interviewed responded to the idea of repatriation with comments that could be considered positive. Many see the Bikinians, as well as other Marshallese, not as premodern natives fitting into nature, but as agents who, if allowed, will defile the natural place through their modern behaviors (driving cars, producing refuse, living in houses rather than huts). Of course, the irony that these individuals themselves live modern lives with automobiles, houses, and disposable products while simultaneously trying to deny Bikinians the same rights because they would ruin a "pristine" nuclear weapons test site somehow escapes them. This blindness, I contend, is a testament to the power of the colonial/military/tourism/environment imaginary that divides the world into a global-scale system of civilized profane spaces and wastelands/wildernesses. It is an imperial spacialization of what practices should occur where and who should perform them. The assumed nature of this dichotomous imaginary obscures for Westerners that most people lack the mobility to cross back and forth between the spaces assigned to modern and premodern activities. It is not that tourists believe the Marshallese should not be able to partake in the activities of making a living in an environment, or to enjoy the trappings of civilized society; it is just that they feel they should not be allowed to do it in the globally prescribed Eden that their tropical islands have been labeled. The fact that it is the only space they have is not given careful consideration. Instead, the naturalness of the place becomes not just something to be viewed but also something to be enforced.

It is here that we see the circular and repeating spirit of coercion, paternalism, and control that underpins the colonialism/militarization/tourism/environment nexus. Places like Bikini and Guam (and Hawaiʻi, Okinawa, Vieques, and so on) are where the seemingly disparate projects of militarization, colonialism, environmental preservation, and tourism combine and espouse a common theme. The message sent, even by well-meaning outsiders, is still clear: "Your island is not your own. It is best managed by someone else." The message intones that the islands are better off, healthier, more beautiful, more useful, and better managed with the paternalistic hand of a colonial power still at the helm, even when that colonial power explodes nuclear weapons on the island or continues condemning land for live-fire training. It is in these contexts that the historically persistent and geographically pervasive spirit of colonial domination rises to the surface and can be more easily viewed. It is also the context from which springs a determined and organized resistance.

CHAPTER 6

Networks of Affinity and Myths of the Postcolonial Pacific

As previous chapters demonstrate, the islands in the imperial margins of the western Pacific have been subjected to intense militarization and colonial practices that aim to control their landscapes, ecologies, politics, and societies. In response, resistance has flared up on these islands, and civil society groups combating militarization have won some major victories: Kahoʻolawe is no longer a bombing range, Makua Valley is no longer used for live-fire training, the planned increased militarization of Guam has been delayed and scaled back, and the construction of a new base in Henoko, Okinawa, has not moved forward. However, as described in chapter 4, these local victories have often resulted in a spatial shift of militarization to islands with less-developed resistance movements. Furthermore, when it comes to blocking or closing military bases, nothing is forever. Many places where bases have been closed, or where permission to site a base has been denied, have later become available again. For example, in 2011 Australia and Singapore had changes of heart and allowed in U.S. military units they had initially refused. Meanwhile, old military areas on Tinian in the Northern Marianas are slated to be reopened. Cam Rahn Bay in Vietnam, an icon of the American presence during the Vietnam War, is now openly discussed as a possible site for U.S. warships. Even the Philippines, which passed a law to outlaw foreign military bases after the closure of the Clark Air Force Base and Subic Bay Naval Base, has been increasing cooperation with the U.S. military and allowing more and more U.S. ships and personnel to visit the archipelago. As tensions between China and U.S. allies in the region have heated up over territorial disputes in the Spratly Islands in the South China Sea and the Senkaku/Diaoyu Islands near Okinawa and Taiwan, some nearby countries have reconsidered distancing themselves from the American military umbrella.

While the U.S. military has tremendous resources and the technical and political ability to shift the military network around the Pacific, activist groups working for demilitarization are not as outmaneuvered in this regional "game" as it may initially appear. The fluidity of both international and local politics means that while not all acts of demilitarization are necessarily permanent victories, it is also true that no act of militarization is permanent. Militarization and the associated changes in the geography of the base network are dynamic processes. As activist groups have learned, constant diligence and pressure must be applied to push back against the constant diligence and pressure of military planners trying to achieve their objectives for maintaining U.S. hegemony in the region. What has become clearer in recent decades is that the campaign to demilitarize and decolonize the Pacific is one without either temporal or spatial borders.

In this chapter I sum up the book's arguments by examining four major themes. The first is to tell the story of two pivotal sites in the production of U.S. hegemony in the post–World War II world: Hiroshima, a well-known site, and Tinian Island in the Northern Mariana Islands (see map 2 in chapter 1), a site that is not well known. In my discussion of these sites, my goal is to draw attention to the uneven geographies of militarization and the connections between bases and battlefields. This chapter's second theme is to demonstrate that even closed military areas, like Tinian, are never free from the possibility of remilitarization. Next, I show how the temporally and spatially dynamic processes of militarization have affected how proponents of demilitarization and decolonization are now operating. In particular, antimilitarization groups have spatially expanded their focus beyond local and regional efforts to form globe-spanning affinity-seeking networks.

Following this discussion of the burgeoning affinity-seeking network, I conclude by discussing the implications this form of political organizing might have for hopes for a more peaceful, decolonized, and secure Pacific. By doing so, I examine how the current operation of hegemony-seeking geopolitics in the region can be subverted and changed. After all, it is not enough to analyze what *has been* going on in the region and the ways in which powerful state actors have imagined and enacted geopolitics. That is only half the equation. In order for the analysis of "what is" to have any value to the struggles going on in the Pacific, it must be linked to what could be. To paraphrase Marx, most geopolitical theorists and planners have only *interpreted* imperial politics in the Pacific, in various ways; the point is to change it.

Tinian/Hiroshima: Considering American Hegemony at Atomic Bomb Pit #2

On Tinian Island there is an old airbase that during World War II was the largest in the world. That was when it was used to enable the bombing of Japan. Today, however, the hastily poured concrete airstrips have mostly crumbled under the shock of the tropical cycling of bright sun and frequent rains. On the edges of the tarmac, the vegetation has almost swallowed the old roads that swirl around it. In contrast to this general pattern of progressive disrepair, there are some areas where both the pavement and vegetation have been managed for continued accessibility. One of these places is the edge of a large tarmac where the B-29 bomber *Enola Gay* backed up over the hole now dubbed "Atomic Bomb Pit #1."

There is a memorial here. An angled glass cage covers the hole that was dug out so that the uranium-impregnated bomb known as "Little Boy" could be hoisted into the low-hanging bomb bay of the American bomber prior to its flight on August 6, 1945. Under its transparent canopy the pit today has pictures on easels showing skinny, pale young men in shorts sweating as they prepared the bomb in the pit before its journey to Hiroshima. It is always dangerous to guess the thoughts of people in photos, but I see in their faces the sense of excitement, of danger, of unease. Were these people unsure of what they were dealing with? Did they understand the momentousness of the tasks they performed? The assembling of the bomb, the delicate painting of the bomb's nose, the raising of the bomb into the plane, the securing of the weapon in its place: did they have a sense of their roles in history?

I am well aware of the debates surrounding the dropping of this bomb. I understand the argument that the dropping of this bomb *may* have saved millions of lives, both American and Japanese, that might have been lost if an invasion of the Japanese mainland had been carried out. Also, the bombing of Hiroshima was not, in its sheer deadliness, very different than the firebombing of Tokyo on March 9, 1945, which killed an estimated one hundred thousand civilians. Knowing this does not make looking at Atomic Bomb Pit #1 any easier.

Unlike many of the military men on Tinian in 1945, I have not had to experience the shock of the bombing of Pearl Harbor and the bloody, ferocious battles on islands across the Pacific where atrocities were committed on the bodies of each other and the islanders whose islands had been invaded. Tinian itself was the site of a brutal battle, after which thousands of Japanese and Okinawan civilians fled to the island's southern end and killed themselves by leaping, often holding their children's hands, over the Suicide Cliffs onto the sea-lapped rocks below. They had been told that the advancing Americans would systematically rape the women and eat the children. Many believed these rumors, and the Japanese military encouraged, and in some cases directly forced, people to commit mass suicide rather than surrender. The dropping of the bomb on Hiroshima was a way to end an epoch of horrendous violence by supplying violence an order of magnitude higher than the usual. The atomic bombing was to be a peak of terror standing above the already tall mountains of constant brutality that had characterized the previous four years of war. In this it succeeded.

I spent a few afternoons and nights sitting near Atomic Bomb Pit #1 in a small clearing containing some well-spaced planted palms and an orange-flowered flame tree. I would watch the vans and rental cars of tourists come to view the pit. They would exit their air-conditioned vehicles and step out into the sticky Tinian air and take turns photographing each other posing in front of the pit. Much could be said about this activity in terms of the colonial/military/tourism/environment nexus, but it is also about getting a souvenir that demonstrates that a person really was there. A photograph verifies that a transformative experience has occurred. She has traveled widely. He has seen sites that matter. They have experienced the energy and aura of an important site, and it has changed them.

For myself, I am not sure how I have been changed by encountering Atomic Bomb Pit #1. I tried to imagine myself as one of those young scrawny men scurrying over the metal body of the weapon, solving technical problems, lifting and placing it in the bomber, being uneasy about the moral implications of what was occurring but maybe feeling like part of something important. Perhaps they were thinking that the violence to come, as incomprehensible as it was, would result in real good. At Atomic Bomb Pit #1 I tried to find empathy for the ghosts in the photographs who were active constructors of the empire to come, but may not have had any idea of what the shape of it would be.

A few days after leaving Tinian I visited the site that is the other side of the story: Hiroshima. As early as May 1943 (long before D-day in Europe) it had been decided that the bomb that would eventually be built and put into Atomic Bomb Pit #1 was going to be used not against Germany, but against the Japanese. The idea that the Japanese were selected for atomic bombing only because the Germans were already out of the war is a myth. Originally, the first atomic bomb was going to be dropped on Chuuk (Truk), a populated Micronesian island that was the anchorage for a large part of the Japanese fleet (demonstrating the oft-repeated American view of Micronesian islands and their native inhabitants as expendable). By the time the bomb was ready, however, much of the Japanese fleet had already been sunk at Chuuk through a conventional air attack in February 1944. Instead, Hiroshima was chosen as the site of the first atomic bomb exploded on people.

As I walked through the Hiroshima Peace Memorial Museum, I was surprised by the first few displays. I expected them to be about life in Hiroshima before the bombing, but the focus was interesting for someone studying militarized places and environments. Having seen many accounts about the bombing of Hiroshima, I came into the museum with some knowledge of the horrors. I thought the first displays would portray the everyday lives of Hiroshima's people and represent the city as a victim of a horrific attack against civilians. I was wrong.

The most noticeable thing about the prebombing displays is that they depict how Japanese militarism and nationalism had permeated the city. There are maps showing where various military barracks were located. There are pictures of the city's populace celebrating in the streets after Japanese victories in China, Southeast Asia, and the Pacific. Particularly poignant is a photo of people joyously cheering the Japanese taking of Nanking, China, in late 1937. In the aftermath of the battle, known as "The Rape of Nanking," Japanese soldiers raped large numbers of women and children and outright slaughtered an estimated two hundred thousand civilians over six weeks. The message in these displays is clear: Hiroshima was not a peaceful city before it was bombed. It was a cog in the Japanese military machine. It supported Japan's aggressive wars both materially and spiritually.

The word that best describes the museum's portrayal of the atomic bombing is *moment* because the museum emphasizes the instantaneous nature of the destruction. At the moment of 8:15 a.m. on August 6 *everything* that existed there melted all at once. In the first hall of the museum are dioramas of the city before and after 8:15 showing the complete destruction of almost all of the buildings in the city, while overhead a film runs on a loop of the bomb dropping from the plane, the bomb exploding, and the mushroom cloud rising above the city. Much of this film was shot from the American bomber that escorted the *Enola Gay* (a bomber that was, revealingly, named *Necessary Evil*). Connecting this moment of destruction to the continuation of the development of nuclear weapons, metal plaques affixed to the walls, etched in Japanese and English, reproduce telegrams the mayors of Hiroshima have sent in protest of every nuclear test conducted by the world's nuclear powers since 1968.

Continuing this theme, upstairs from the first hall are displays focusing on the development of nuclear weapons since the bombing of Hiroshima. Descriptions of modern nuclear weapons systems demonstrate how much larger the current hydrogen bombs are than the fission bomb dropped on Hiroshima. In this room there is also a giant model globe with missiles protruding from it to show the numbers of nuclear warheads in the world. Nearby is a helpful graph showing that the United States and Russia each maintain close to ten thousand nuclear warheads. Other countries, including the UK, France, and China, are listed with their hundreds of weapons. The displays here also depict the history of nuclear testing, nuclear accidents, near accidents, and crises when there were threats of nuclear weapons being used.

The next part of the museum, however, is the hardest one to walk through.

It is a view of the bombing from the scale of everyday life and a demonstration of what a nuclear bomb does to bodies. The museum re-creates the atmosphere of life in Hiroshima after the bomb struck. The low, reddish lighting starts as you walk down a hallway dominated by pictures of the mushroom cloud taken from the ground from various vantage points around the city. Then the hallway opens into a series of smallish rooms. In the rooms are wax statues of children with flesh melting off their bodies as fires burn in broken buildings. Blocks of concrete show the silhouettes left behind when the bomb vaporized a person and the stone was scorched all around the crouching victim. The displays also include all sorts of watches stopped at 8:15. There are photos of people who had the pattern of their clothes burned into their flesh: darker colors absorbing the heat and scorching their designs into the backs of women. Artwork drawn by survivors adorns the walls: of burning bodies limply hanging over bridges as people died attempting to jump into the city's rivers; of the skeleton of a family member left standing with the flesh burned off, captioned with the sorrowful regret that the artist was not there to attempt to save her ("I'm so sorry, it must have been very hot"). There are detailed descriptions and pictures of the various stages of radiation sickness: children with hair falling out, men with large purple sores around their necks.

There is also an emphasis on the bomb's effects on children. There are narratives about children heroically saved from the firestorm only to bloat and die days later from radiation poisoning. There are details about Sadako Sasaki, who was one mile from the explosion at the age of two. Although she was growing up into an athletic young woman, she developed leukemia at age twelve. Believing that if she folded one thousand paper cranes she would be cured, she started folding the cranes and died. There are also displays of children's possessions: a scorched lunch box opened to reveal the ashes of a meal packed for a boy's lunch, a special shoe that—when found by the girl's mother—was the only confirmation that the girl had been killed, a three-year-old's burned and twisted tricycle that was buried with the child because her parents could not bear to think that their daughter would have nothing to play with after her death.

As tragic as the day of August 6, 1945, was in Hiroshima, we should remember that museum displays are as much about the present as about the past. What, then, is the message from the Hiroshima Peace Memorial Museum? While the theme of "never again" is certainly prominent, there is another message here about militarism. As the displays at the front of the museum emphasize, the people of Hiroshima were supporters of a militarized society. This museum is a political message for the present, a not-so-subtle suggestion to Japanese visitors to resist the ongoing efforts to remilitarize Japan. To people from other parts of

FIGURE 9. Atomic Bomb Pit #2 on Tinian Island. Photo by author.

the world, particularly Americans, the message is not subtle either. The message is not, as some might assume, that Americans are inherently violent or owing apologies. Instead, the message reads something like this: We were once militarily strong; we used our might against others to benefit the military, the politicians, and their corporate appendages. One day our empire declined, as happens with all empires, and we reaped what we sowed. The violence we had so patriotically embraced when it was directed against others was turned back onto us. Then the mushroom cloud came and we were vaporized, burned, irradiated, broken.

At the end of my visit to the museum, I began recalling something from a few days before, when I was on Tinian. On the east side of the tarmac is Atomic Bomb Pit #2. At this site, on the early morning of August 9, 1945, the bomb destined for Nagasaki was loaded onto an airplane by people, many of the same ones who loaded the first bomb onto the *Enola Gay*. This time they knew exactly what they were doing. I remembered the photos propped up on displays in Atomic Bomb Pit #2 and realized this site marked not just the end of a war, but the beginning of an American project of hegemony that—when examined at a human scale from *within* the region—can easily be seen as an exercise not of liberation, but of domination.

War Machine in the Marianas Redux: Resurrecting Closed Military Sites

With the close of World War II, the base at Tinian was made redundant. Airfields closer to Asia, like Okinawa, became more important sites for the projection of American airpower. The northern third of Tinian, including the atomic bomb pits, stayed in the hands of the military and has hosted some small-scale exercises over the years. The middle third of the island is still under military jurisdiction but was for a time leased to local people. The southern third, with the city of San Jose and about three thousand people, is the civilian zone. Although for a time militarization subsided on the island and moved to other sites in the island Pacific, it does not appear to be staying that way. As military units are being slated to move to nearby Guam, Tinian is seen as a site for some of the training that cannot be conducted on heavily populated and increasingly resistant Guam. Some of the plans for training on the island are truly extensive.

While I was doing research in Guam and the Northern Marianas, I had a great deal of difficulty getting in touch with the higher-ranked military officers responsible for organizing the buildup. This difficulty was hardly surprising, but it was nevertheless frustrating. And then one morning, while I was eating in a small restaurant on Tinian, the Marine general and navy captain leading the development of the buildup in Guam and the Northern Marianas walked in to have a meeting with Tinian's mayor. The men were sitting with some of the mayor's aides, but the mayor was not yet there. I introduced myself by saying I was studying the military buildup in Guam and the Northern Marianas. I said I had done previous research in Vieques, Puerto Rico, and was now looking at the future plans for Guam and Tinian. Mentioning Vieques was evidently a mistake. It immediately put the general and captain ill at ease. I probably should have proceeded cautiously. I sensed, however, the mayor would probably come in shortly, and in the brief time I had I bluntly asked the one question that had been most on my mind. I had seen in obscure (but technically public) documents that the military planned to regularly fire artillery from Tinian at Aguiguan (Goat Island) just to the south of Tinian. The geography of the military landholdings on Tinian is such that there were only two real possibilities. Either the military planned to fire the artillery over the top of the inhabited section of southern Tinian (or the artillery shells would follow paths *very* close to the inhabited shore areas), or they were going to try to acquire more land on the southern end of the island. Furthermore, I was surprised by the plan because Aguiguan is a treasure trove of cultural artifacts. It was the island where the native Chamorros made their final stand against Spanish domination, and archaeologists report that it is suitable for listing on the National Registry of Historic Places.

Knowing this, I asked, "Why are you planning to use Goat Island as a target, and where exactly do you plan to fire the artillery from?" This evidently was a really wrong thing to say. The mayor's aides looked up from their conversation, and the U.S. military officers were peeved and defensive. The two officers looked at each other, and then the captain offered, "Look, we don't know about that plan yet. There may be problems with civilian airline routes. It's too premature to talk about that plan."

So that was that. I tried to follow up with them numerous times, but they never responded. When interviewing municipal officials on Tinian, I asked them if they had heard of the plan. They had not. I asked them what they thought of the possibility that the majority of Tinian and its surrounding waters might be made off-limits to the people. They responded that people would be really upset, but none of the U.S. military officials had brought up the possibility of that occurring. Archaeological surveys had already been completed at the military's request, showing (in extensive detail) exactly what parts of the island would be affected by the new military training. The impact area was almost the whole island. The U.S. military, however, had not made the island's government or its people aware of what was coming. This, unfortunately, is standard operating procedure for the military. They often do not release information until the plans are well under way or until the environmental impact statement process compels them to.

Like most militarized islands, there are those who oppose the militarization and those who support it. Some of the people I spoke with on Tinian were looking forward to the possible economic stimulus the military training might bring. Others, however, said that they remembered the Vietnam War era, when B-52s returning from Southeast Asia would drop their leftover bombs on Aguiguan before landing on Guam. The bombs would rain down around Tinian and explode just offshore from San Jose. People told me that as kids they would meet in the morning following such bombings, sharing how many loud explosions had woken them. Just as on Guam, Vieques, Hawai'i, and many other islands, clearly some of the people on Tinian did not support a return to the days of intensive military activity around their island. The plans, however, are in place for that return regardless. While the plan to shell Aguiguan from Tinian has been shelved, extensive environmental impact statements have been prepared for the return of other kinds of military training.

As mentioned, Tinian is not the only former military site in the region that could experience a return of the U.S. military. Pagan Island in the Northern

Marianas is also earmarked for live-fire military exercises. Outside of the Marianas, the most notable location rumored to be a site for increased U.S. military use is Subic Bay in the Philippines. Subic Bay was once the largest U.S. naval base outside the United States. The base, notorious for both chemical contamination and high levels of prostitution in nearby Olongapo (Enloe, 1990), has recently been visited by U.S. senators and other officials interested in discussing a return. Furthermore, in a quest for more economic development, the mayor of Olongapo has been lobbying the U.S. and Philippine governments to allow the U.S. military to return to Subic. Women's groups in Olongapo and near the former Clark Air Base, while hoping the military will not return, are bracing for the possibility.

This spatial shifting of the military around the region, to both old bases and new ones, is a major challenge facing demilitarization activists. After all, many of these groups are local groups, fighting local battles. Even though they are sometimes successful in those struggles, either limiting the military or driving them out of their islands completely, there has been an increasing recognition that one island's victory can often become another one's burden.

The Perils and Promise of Multiscalar Activism

The Pentagon's ability to reorganize its network regionally and globally in response to local and national resistances has caused antimilitarization groups to reformulate the scales on which they operate. As one Hawai'i activist noted, "We cannot just fight on one level, because this will just move the opposition to another level" (Becker, 2007). As a result, regional and global organizations have begun to play a larger role in antimilitarization activism. On the regional level, groups in places like Latin America and the Asia Pacific have gathered activists together to make pronouncements such as the following by the Asia-Pacific Consultation of Movements against U.S. Military Bases in 2006: "They try to trick us saying, 'this is for your security.' But experience has shown clearly enough that the U.S. military presence, far from protecting the people, only violates people's sovereignty, destroys local people's cultural and economic life, brings on violence against women and children, and disaster to the environment."

On the global level, at the 2004 World Social Forum in Mumbai activists from militarized places around the world formed a new organization, called simply "No Bases," dedicated to the abolishment of all foreign military bases in the world. This network put together its own global conference in March 2007 in Quito, Ecuador, where hundreds of activists gathered to formalize the network. The goals of this group were released in a communiqué at the conference that stated: "We call for the total abolition of all foreign military bases and all other infrastructure used for wars of aggression, including military operations, maneuvers, trainings, exercises, agreements, weapons in space, military laboratories and other forms of military interventions. We demand an end to both the construction of new bases and the reinforcement of existing bases; an end to and cleanup of environmental contamination; an end to legal immunity and other privileges of foreign military personnel. We demand integral restoration and full and just compensation for social and environmental damages caused by these bases."

How, though, do groups and activists who have generally focused on resisting the violences of militarization in the places and on the scales of everyday living move their activism to the regional and global scale? The U.S. military operates as an entity with a global reach, and on one level activists recognize that they can be more successful by matching that scale. But how do they negotiate how to act at a variety of scales to achieve their objectives? The spatial imaginary of the No Bases network was summed up in their declaration, "Realizing that Empire wants to rule globally, we have come together to pool our strength on a global scale to protect people's lives and wellbeing against the U.S. military system" (posted on http://nobasesnetwork.blogspot.com/). To put this ethic into operation, the group started an email list to connect activist groups from around the world and to share news of military projects and operations as well as stories of resistance. Also, like other contemporary activist organizations striving to link spatially scattered struggles and to raise awareness of those struggles, the organization started a website (Fluri, 2006). The website has been used to connect groups and to present their struggles to a wider audience. Also, it has been a way of discursively framing their local struggles as similar to each other, and as in need of worldwide solidarity. Furthermore, the site was used to make people in the network aware of events, such as the 2007 global conference in Quito. The No Bases network has somewhat fizzled in the years following the conference, however, for reasons I discuss below. Regardless, I believe there is much that can be learned by examining this example of global-scale organizing.

I attended the Quito conference as an observer and participant. The conference, attended by over four hundred people, was designed to have two "streams": one with sessions about local struggles and another devoted to constructing the organization. I attended the second stream, in which people focused on determining the shape of the network, establishing its goals, deciding how those goals would be accomplished, and plotting future events and actions. These discussions took place over three days. Conference attendees divided into three groups of approximately twenty people each; each group discussed a cer-

FIGURE 10. Posters from Japanese and Korean groups at the No Bases Conference in Quito, Ecuador, 2007. Photo by author.

tain aspect of the organization. Later, the three groups met together to hash out agreements or compromises on the different visions that came out of each group.

In these sessions many of the debates centered on issues of scale. Activists were generally pragmatic and recognized that to be effective the "global" organization would need to operate in different ways at different scales. Of course, scales are not pre-existing categories but are produced through discourses and actions (Marston, 2000). Activists generally spoke about strategies for action at the common "local," "national," "regional," and "global" scales. While most activists agreed on these somewhat traditional conceptualizations of scale, the ways in which this global organization should function in and across these scales was the subject of much debate. Some of the more contentious discussions illuminate how activists engaged with questions of scale.

First, there was some disagreement over how centralized the organization's decision-making power ought to be. Second, there were debates over the discursive framing of antimilitarization struggles. Should they be represented as local struggles against in-place violences or pieces of a global anti-imperialist struggle? Last, there was significant disagreement over the role of nationalism and the pursuit of sovereignty in antimilitarization movements. In other words, was the global movement against *all* military bases, all *foreign* military bases, or just U.S. bases?

In terms of how the movement should be organized, participants came to a general consensus that the organization should be a horizontally organized, nonhierarchical "network" of autonomous local struggles rather than a more centrally directed "coalition." It was felt that the global network should be used to serve the local struggles. Activists saw the job of the global organization as one of support for local groups. The network should provide research and information about the global movements of military activities and alert other groups around the globe when a particular group was facing a decisive moment and needed solidarity. They generally agreed that the decisions regarding actions, however, should be made by local groups, or by the network only through a consensus of the local groups.

There was some opposition to this emphasis on the autonomy of local groups from different quarters. A few participants felt, on ideological grounds, that a stronger, centralized organization would be more effective. Delegates from places with undeveloped (or nonexistent) resistance movements were the most concerned. With only a handful of attendees at the conference representing groups from Africa (including Diego Garcia/Mauritius), they were concerned that local struggles against increasing U.S. militarization in their region would be hard to mount without substantial outside organization and support. Furthermore, it was noted that the conference did not even have any delegates from some of the most critical occupied and devastated parts of the world, such as the Middle East and Central Asia.[1] It was suggested that one of the global network's roles would be to try to connect with groups from these regions and to play an active role in developing and supporting new groups in these places.

Conference attendees also deliberated about whether the global organization should provide a guiding discursive framework for local struggles. There were suggestions that local groups should rhetorically frame the militarization of their communities in global terms. Local groups, some attendees insisted, should attempt to "connect the dots" and see their local situation in the context of the imperial present, and to see their local struggle as linked to the global struggle against not just militarization but *militarism* and imperialism. Some activists also felt that it was important to have banners for the global movement at local protests to demonstrate the linkages among the struggles.

This idea of rhetorically "scaling up" the resistance to local militarization was not embraced by all of the groups present at the meeting. As mentioned, military bases are both the sites from which violence is projected through military force into combat zones and the places at which local violences are dispersed into host communities. Many activists see these types of violences as linked and mutually reinforcing, and this perspective forms a basis of solidarity among many activists at the conference. There are, however, some differences of opinions. Activists that emphasized bases as sites of the projection of violence had little problem linking local struggles with a global view of the entire war-producing network. Some groups focusing on local base impacts, however, were reluctant to embrace an explicitly anti-imperialist label. Some of the delegations from Japan, for example, felt that many members of their broad-based local coalitions against U.S. bases would not agree with, or want to identify with, an explicitly anti-imperialist agenda. Like the example set by the Vieques protest movement, some members of these delegations felt that their protests could be more successful if they were able to forge politically broad movements in place.

In the end, conference pronouncements shied away from openly using the language of "anti-imperialism" while still emphasizing international solidarity. I believe that researchers and activists should not see this focus on solidarity coupled with a reluctance to label the movement as "anti-imperialist" as a contradiction between action based on specifically local struggles ("militant particularisms") on the one hand and global, more orthodox political strategies on the other (Harvey, 1996). Instead, the activists decided to use scale in a much more nuanced and pragmatic way in terms of how they represented their struggles. The local groups attending the conference seemed quite willing to give local groups the ability to craft their own *representations* of the local struggles in order to build broad local coalitions. If representing a struggle as part of a global anti-imperialist struggle could help a group in a particular local political context, then they could pursue that strategy. If that position could be detrimental to building local alliances, then they could downplay it or omit it from representations of the struggle. Working within these politically broad autonomous movements, however, core members would maintain connections with the global solidarity network and keep one eye on the "big picture" of how their protest movements fit into the global scene. In other words, the people in the local movements who are connected to the global network are almost undoubtedly anti-imperialist, though they may not represent their groups, or themselves, that way in their local context for strategic reasons.

Perhaps the most contentious debates at the conference dealt with the use of the national scale. In particular, there were many conversations about how sovereignty and nationalism should be used as platforms for antimilitarization struggles. Researchers have noted that social movements operating at multiple scales have used the scale of the nation-state to redress more global concerns (Glassman, 2001; McCarthy, 2005). This is partly because, unlike many global processes directed by unrepresentative entities such as the U.S. military, World

Bank, IMF, and G20, most contemporary nation-states are viewed as operating, at least nominally, in a democratic fashion. In theory, then, on the national scale, activists might find that the U.S. military can be held accountable for actions within another nation's sovereign territory. Of course, there is a large amount of variation among states and their views about U.S. imperial power. For instance, delegates at the conference from Ecuador, Venezuela, and Cuba who have left-leaning administrations professed national sovereignty as a potent weapon against U.S. bases. During the conference, the newly elected president of Ecuador, Rafael Correa, affirmed that his government would expel the United States from its base in Manta when the lease expired in 2009 (he also publicly quipped that he would allow the United States to stay in Manta only if the United States gave Ecuador a base in Miami). Activists clearly saw that putting pressure on national governments, or having allies at the scale of the nation-state, could be a very effective way to resist the imposition of U.S. bases in their localities.

Some activists at the conference sought to use the concept of national sovereignty as a bulwark against foreign bases in a different way. As the theme of this book suggests, many U.S. bases are located in places with colonial political statuses. Delegates representing Guam, Puerto Rico, Diego Garcia, and Hawai'i were explicit about the mutually reinforcing connection between hosting U.S. military bases and the lack of political self-determination. While the colonial statuses of these places differ to some degree, activists from these localities felt that struggles for political sovereignty were inseparable from the fight against U.S. bases. In these cases, a spatial reorganization of legal sovereignty in the form of a local national state was seen as a powerful mechanism for fighting against the militarization of their places.

Other activists at the conference, however, were concerned about a focus on nationalism and sovereignty as a protection against American militarism. Delegates from nations in Europe and Japan cautioned that right-wing elements in those countries could render calling for nationalism and sovereignty not only ineffective for fighting against U.S. bases, but possibly dangerous. One delegate from Germany stated that many members of the German right fully supported calling for the expulsion of U.S. troops from German bases in the name of sovereignty and nationalism, but their aim was to strengthen a dangerous German nationalist militarism. Also, these delegates pointed out that NATO bases, British bases, French bases, Russian bases, and domestic American bases were also sites of violence and contamination, and so the organization's focus should not be just on "foreign" or U.S. overseas bases. There was some lively debate about whether the activist network should be calling for the abolition of "foreign military bases" or just "military bases" in general. Furthermore, the exclusionary nature of many forms of nationalism, as well as the often patriarchal forms it takes, struck many people at the conference as a counterproductive way to address issues of militarization. In the end, the participants agreed that nationalism and sovereignty could be used strategically but cautiously. While the network agreed that its focus should be on *foreign* military bases, some participants were still uneasy with this. One of the conference organizers commented, "cautiously, the network treaded the fine line between self-determination and chauvinism" (No Bases email communiqué, March 14, 2007).

Although the conference in Quito was an important moment for anti-imperialist and antimilitarization organizing, the follow-up has been weak. The No Bases network has continued to operate, and activists have met at World Social Forums—as well as at regional and national conferences—but there has not been a lot of follow-up at the global level. Proposals for a global day of action at military sites across the world were not adopted at the conference over concerns that it could not be successfully pulled off. The conference did, however, successfully reaffirm the importance of thinking globally about activism in militarized communities. By "connecting the dots" of communities affected by military bases, the No Bases organization brought activists together from across the world who now stay in touch through less formal networks. These activists still share surveillance of the activities of the globe-spanning U.S. military and maintain networks of solidarity with each other.

Transcending Hegemony

What has been put in motion by organizations such as No Bases and other regional antimilitarization groups is not a movement for colonized places to gain more power vis-à-vis world powers, but rather a radical reimagining of power itself. It is a project whose aim is to move away from politics based on hegemony toward expanding circles of affinity. Contradicting the pundits, governments, military planners, and traditional geopolitical theoreticians on both sides of the Pacific, social movements in the Pacific are evolving whose aims are not to support one hegemonic power or another, but rather to transcend hegemony and domination as the organizing principles of international politics. The rationale for this strategy is part tactical and part ethical. On the tactical level, the colonized islands of the Pacific cannot turn the tables and win a battle of hegemony and domination. The idea that North America could be ruled from Honolulu or Asia from Tinian is clearly impractical and unreasonable. Undercutting the operation of hegemony in the region is really the only practical option for self-determination.

Pursuing decolonization through affinity is also a far stronger political strategy because it invites inclusion. By rejecting both militarization and colonization—which are fundamentally about dominating others through the use (or credible threat) of violence—social movements in the Pacific can expand supportive networks based on affinity and fueled in part by the philosophy's ethical nature. Namely, the philosophy is one not of chauvinism for a particular nationality or in-group (or for the "exceptionalism" of one imperial power or another), but one of inclusion, equality, and self-determination that lends it universal appeal and legitimacy. In other words, the political goal is for island groups "to recover, establish or enhance their ability to determine the conditions of *their own* existence, while allowing and encouraging others to do the same" (Day, 2005, p. 13, emphasis in original).

Several factors need to be taken into account when examining the growth of this regional (and global) movement for transcending hegemony. First, the ethics of self-determination and international affinity are historically deep projects. Hegemony-seeking power that aims to build hierarchy and affinity-seeking power that aims to level it are not creatures of different epochs in human history. Rather, they have both always existed, they continue to exist, and they will always exist (see, for instance, James Scott's [2009] brilliant work in Southeast Asia). There is no moment or "revolution" to end the contest between affinity and hegemony. The quest for both is always present. In any social milieu there are always social practices that enhance affinity and ones that enhance domination and hegemony. Therefore, to produce a global politics based on affinity you do not have to start from scratch and find something new. Social relations based on affinity exist now: in our daily lives, in homes and schools, and in globe-spanning networks. Even if it appears, over many scales, to be subordinate to the flows of hegemony-seeking power, it is there. The goal, then, for those who seek an affinity-based international order is not to "start" something, but to seek out, valorize, and promote affinity-growing social processes and make them thrive, grow, and expand the spaces in which their principles dominate. As mentioned in the introduction to this book, there is a legacy to draw from for imagining geopolitics according to the principles of equality and mutual aid. While theorists like Kropotkin (1885), who espouse European concepts of anarchism and mutual aid, are one source, there is also a rich theoretical tradition from indigenous Pacific scholars who draw upon Pacific cultural practices of aloha and island connectivity and solidarity (Hau'ofa, 1994; Lilomaiava-Doktor, 2009; Teaiwa, 2000; Shigematsu & Camacho, 2010; Wilson, 2000). There is also a strong tradition of networked regional activism, as demonstrated by the Nuclear Free and Independent Pacific movement and the "Moana Nui" conferences in 2011 and 2013 (http://mnaa-ca.org/).

Another factor to take into account when examining the project of transcending hegemony is the role of destroying old myths and producing new ones. As I have tried to demonstrate throughout this book, supported by the scholarship of others (Agnew, 2009; Shields, 1991; Wright, 2006), myths are powerful forces for governing actions and for determining what is imaginable and allowable. To produce a different kind of politics in the region, different myths for the Pacific need to be developed and promoted. A rhetorical battle must be waged that takes a hatchet to many myths in the Pacific. The Pacific is not empty. The Pacific is not paradise. The Pacific is not a wasteland. The Pacific is not already *post*colonial. The Pacific is not small. The Pacific is not dependent. The Pacific is not the tip of someone else's spear. The Pacific is not someone else's borderland. In place of these old, mistaken myths, new myths must be sown. The Pacific is big. Affinity and solidarity can triumph. Self-determination and self-governance are possible and practical. The islands in the Pacific are not just the edges of someone else's empire, but their own center.

To transcend hegemony in the region, there is a need not only to nurture and promote the values of affinity within the region but to geographically expand them as well. This is part of Richard Day's (2005) concept of "infinite responsibility." Given that the primary states involved in the contest for hegemony are the United States and China (see chapter 1), to successfully supplant the hegemonic battle between those powers on the edges of the Pacific, there is an urgent need for Pacific social movements to reach out with education and solidarity to groups in China, the United States, and beyond. The Pacific needs to be represented as a place of life, not just as a militarized logistics space of global trade or the site of someone else's profit-seeking "vital system," so that citizens, policy makers, politicians, and others around the world come to see and treat the space differently. Concurrently, solid social movement organizing must also reach out to people on both sides of the Pacific.

Pacific groups attempting to reach out to civil society groups in China and the United States face challenges, but doing so in both places is critical. Several activists I have spoken with have commented that it is sometimes difficult to make linkages with women's and peace groups from China because the activities of some purportedly activist groups are controlled and surveilled by the Chinese government. Change may be on the horizon, however. While the Communist Party of China (CCP) remains firmly in political power, the state's grip over civil society has gradually loosened over the past decades (Guthrie, 2008). While the Chinese state still retains strong censorship capabilities and militarized institutions of social control, there have been tremendous changes in Chinese society that could lead to a substantial erosion of state control and open a crucial window for linkages of affinity and solidarity between Pacific and Chinese citizens.

While it may be challenging for American audiences to recognize this, from the Pacific perspective the more difficult and intractable problem government in the region has historically been not China but the United States. China may have a nondemocratic government with a long history of human rights abuses, but what has China done to the people and landscapes of the island Pacific compared with the United States? There may be reason to fear the dictatorial nature of the Chinese state run by the CCP, but if the United States were to draw down military forces in the region, there is no evidence that China would engage the islands with similar colonial policies as those of the United States, fascist-era Japan, or former European colonial powers.

The United States, on the other hand, is a known entity. The nation has a century-long history of colonial control and militarization in the region as well as an unambiguous stated desire to continue it indefinitely. Furthermore, unlike in China, there are few signs that substantial political change is on the horizon in the United States—at least change that is relevant to the islands on the empires' edge. U.S. policy toward the island Pacific has been remarkably consistent for over a hundred years. From McKinley to Teddy Roosevelt, from Truman to Reagan, from George W. Bush to Barack Obama: few U.S. administrations have sought to rein in the U.S. military's global operations, and none have seriously made moves to dismantle U.S. colonial and military control over the island Pacific. The few contemporary American politicians who have suggested dismantling the U.S. Pacific Baseworld tend to be on either the right or left margins of American politics (for example, Ron Paul and Dennis Kucinich). While these views may be politically marginal, they do demonstrate that there is some public support for curbing U.S. militarization in the Pacific (even if mostly due to concerns over the extensive financial costs).

Activists in the Pacific have been keenly aware that decolonization and demilitarization in the region depend on solidarity and support from outside the region. As I described in chapter 2, one of the problems with getting the U.S. government to change its activities in the Pacific is that so few U.S. citizens are aware of what is occurring in the region. Many of the activists I have met over the course of my research have noted that one of the most important first steps toward a demilitarized future is educating people both inside and outside the region about what is happening here. It has certainly been my personal experience that once people are aware of what is occurring in the region, they are more likely to be supportive of the aims of self-determination and demilitarization. While there are challenges in building bridges within the Pacific region and with citizens in the United States, China, Japan, South Korea, and other Pacific Rim countries, doing so is really the only long-term solution to the current tensions and militarization of the region. What is needed is an ever-expanding circle of affinity that focuses on the common desires we have as people, whether in Hawai'i, Okinawa, Guam, New York, Shanghai, or Hiroshima.

How, though, does the region move from a bristling militarized borderland to a region of affinity? How does the politically fractured region move toward an integration that goes beyond merely a shared integration into the capitalist world market? With such a dynamic and broad region, the answer lies not so much in a rigid political program as in the fluid creation of strategies driven by the insight that hegemony is an outdated political mode of thinking that can be transcended. In other words, to create a region organized by a geopolitics of peace, there is not so much a road map to follow as a guiding ethic: the ethic of universal affinity.

Is this vision of a more peaceful, demilitarized, decolonized Pacific just a utopian dream? While it will obviously take some effort to make the vision real, discounting the possibility of an affinity-based geopolitics in the Pacific is wrong for two reasons: one moral and one analytical. First, it is difficult to defend the morality of "realist" views that consider inevitable the status quo of a world organized hierarchically and premised on violence, domination, exploitation, and the continued creation of whole populations of sacrificial "bare life." Following from J. K. Gibson-Graham's (2008) argument that scholars need to be more focused on discovering possibilities for emancipatory political projects than on explaining why larger structural forces will always crush them, I believe that there is a moral imperative for scholars, teachers, activists, and citizens to explore new, alternative visions when current ones are causing misery.

Analytically, it is also a mistake to discount the possibility of an affinity-seeking geopolitics in the Asia-Pacific region. The idea may be practiced only in small pockets surrounded by a larger system of hegemony-seeking violence produced by powerful states (backed by the legitimizing power of think tanks, planners, pundits, and politicians), but history shows that these are the conditions under which most new social orders have begun. Capitalism was once just an idea in a sea of other forms of social relations. So too was the idea of the nation-state. So too was the idea that human races are equal. As David Harvey (2005) convincingly details, even neoliberalism—the dominant political economic paradigm of the early twenty-first century—was only decades ago a "utopian" idea.

The idea of an affinity-seeking geopolitics in the Pacific should not be discounted because of the supposed "smallness" of where it comes from, either. What happens in small places can have big effects. History has amply shown that what happens in the islands of the Pacific affects global balances of power and can tip the scales of planetary hegemony. The islands of Asia and the Pacific have been the sites of epic battles and conflicts between empires. From World

War II to the Cold War to current standoffs between the United States, China, and North Korea, these islands have been the staging grounds for intense militarization, nuclear experimentation, and potentially planet-decimating warfare of all kinds. Is it so hard to believe that they can also be the sites where the seeds can be planted for an international politics that rejects relationships of domination? Or is it easier to imagine the end of the world than the end of hegemony?

NOTES

Chapter 1. Hegemony and Affinity in the Islands of Empire

1. Other scholars have used similar terms, such as *alter-geopolitics* (Koopman, 2011) and *anti-geopolitics* (Ó Tuathail, 1996), but I have chosen to use *affinity geopolitics* because the term evokes not just what the perspective critiques (traditional geopolitics) but also what it promotes (affinity-seeking forms of international relations).

2. These "rights" or "privileges" associated with being part of the protected body of the polity should not be thought of as positive in nature. As Foucault, Agamben, and other theorists point out, being part of this in-group makes one subject to a wide array of coercive technologies that aim to make the population docile, productive, and exploitable for capital accumulation. While being cast out from the realm of state protections can leave someone vulnerable to all sorts of abuses and death, living within them is not without problems.

3. See also Grugel (2004) for discussion of how networked NGOs and state power interact in the Asian context.

4. Karatani (2008) discusses capital-nation-state as an interlocking triad of capital (exploitative market relations), nation (bounded and xenophobic relationships of mutual aid), and state (hierarchical government). He posits that this triad can be overcome through the creation of what he refers to as "X," which is a system based on the expansion of a nonexclusionary system of mutual aid and free association.

5. The ethic of affinity seeking is espoused by authors including Epeli Hau'ofa (1994), Rob Wilson (2000), Cynthia Enloe (2007), and Catherine Lutz (2009).

Chapter 2. Surveying the Baseworld

1. See Military Toxics Project, www.miltoxproj.org.

Chapter 3. Seeing like an Empire

1. The information presented in this chapter stems from research I conducted in the Marshall Islands in 2001, 2002, and 2007, as well as from a review of previous social science research and popular magazine accounts dealing with Bikini Atoll. I studied historical conceptualizations of Bikini Atoll published over the past six decades and ascertained the current attitudes of various groups of people toward the atoll. During stays on Bikini Atoll, Majuro Atoll, and Kili Island I conducted semistructured interviews with tourists, resort management and workers, Department of Energy personnel, Republic of the Marshall Islands government officials, and members of the Bikinian community

and government to analyze their interactions with, and conceptualizations of, Bikini. I supplemented this information with a review of recent tourist-oriented periodical articles and newspaper stories from the United States about current development activities on Bikini Atoll. I also studied local representations of Bikini from two years (2001 and 2002) of the *Marshall Islands Journal* (a newspaper based in Majuro, Marshall Islands) as well as information provided on the web page maintained by Jack Niedenthal, Trust Liaison to the People of Bikini. I pieced together past conceptualizations of the atoll by consulting written academic accounts and articles about Bikini Atoll in American periodicals published from 1946 to the present.

2. See the movie *Half-Life*.

3. The Pacific is not the only region where places are subjected to these traveling place-myths. For example, see Shields (1991) for discussions of the Canadian "North" and Waitt and Head's (2002) discussion of the Kimberley Mountains in Australia.

4. The publicity, photographs, and film accounts of the tests also served the domestic political purposes of normalizing atomic testing and militarization. See Kirsch (1997).

5. For a complete listing of the ships sunk at Bikini, and the whereabouts of the ships that survived, see Delgado, Lenihan, & Murphy (1991); Delgado (1996); and Niedenthal (2001).

6. The United States eventually detonated approximately one thousand nuclear weapons on the mainland, mostly in Nevada but also in Utah and Mississippi and at other sites. It is obvious they overcame their earlier reluctance to test the weapons in the continental United States.

7. See Naomi Klein's (2007) book *The shock doctrine: The rise of disaster capitalism*.

8. This portrayal of the Marshall Islands as anchored aircraft carriers is used in a mural in the airport on Kwajalein Atoll.

9. See, for example, the *National Geographic* article on Bikini in 1946 (Markwith, 1946). The documentary film *Radio Bikini*, produced by Robert Stone in 1988 (which was nominated for an academy award), also shows in vivid detail how the military's meetings with the Bikinians were staged and reshot numerous times.

10. "Juda" is the name of the Bikinians' iroij (leader) in 1946.

11. While the two American portrayals of Bikini, as a nonplace and as a marginalized place, may not necessarily be logically consistent, they were used in a complementary manner to conceptualize Bikini as an experimental space, effectively legitimizing the use of atomic weapons there.

12. For a more detailed discussion of the connections between the bathing suit and Bikini Atoll, as well as a theoretical analysis of the similar marginalization and exoticizing of women's bodies and Bikinians, see Teaiwa (2000).

Chapter 4. Local Resistances and Imperial Reactions

1. See also the movie *Act of War* on the overthrow.

2. See website for DMZ Hawai'i for up-to-date information on military activities in Hawai'i.

Chapter 5. Colonialism, Militarization, Tourism, and Environment as Nexus

1. The *Nagato* was formerly Japanese admiral Yamamoto's flagship, from which the attack on Pearl Harbor was commanded. The other major ships in Bikini's lagoon include the destroyer USS *Anderson*, submarine USS *Apogon*, destroyer USS *Lamson*, merchant vessel USS *Carlisle*, submarine USS *Pilotfish*, and the Japanese warship HIJMS *Sakawa*.

2. Bikini is not the only former bombing range to be considered as a possible national park. See also Misrach (1990).

3. In 2001 the total profits distributed was $250,000.

4. Moruroa is an atoll in French Polynesia that the French have used for nuclear weapons testing.

5. CERCLA stands for the Comprehensive Environmental Response, Compensation, and Liability Act, which deals with the cleanup of sites contaminated by industry and U.S. government agencies (including the military).

6. U.S. courts ruled that U.S. military installations in foreign countries are not protected by American environmental laws. See the court case *Arc Ecology v. United States Department of the Air Force* discussed in Stasch (2006).

Chapter 6. Networks of Affinity and Myths of the Postcolonial Pacific

1. While this was not brought up at the conference, there is an organization in the Middle East and Central Asia that is also organized as a loose network and that developed in response to American military activities and the local and national impacts of U.S. bases: Al Qaeda. No doubt any suggested similarities between the No Bases network and Al Qaeda would make conference participants extremely uncomfortable due to the fact that the No Bases network is firmly committed to nonviolence. Further research on resistance to U.S. militarization, however, should attempt to deal with this question of why there is an obvious geography to the forms of resistance. Why has the No Bases network sprung from local nonviolent resistance movements in Latin America, Europe, Japan, Korea, the Philippines, the United States and its colonies, with no representation from Middle Eastern and Central Asian groups? Why has a violent reaction occurred in other places?

REFERENCES

Agamben, G. (1993). *The coming community*. Minneapolis: University of Minnesota Press.

Agamben, G. (1998). *Homo sacer*. Stanford: Stanford University Press.

Agamben, G. (2005). *State of exception*. Chicago: University of Chicago Press.

Agnew, J. (1993). The United States and American hegemony. In P. Taylor (Ed.), *Political geography of the twentieth century: A global analysis* (pp. 207–238). London: Belhaven.

Agnew, J. (2005). *Hegemony: The new shape of global power*. Philadelphia: Temple University Press.

Agnew, J. (2009). *Globalization and sovereignty*. New York: Rowman & Littlefield.

Aguon, J. (2005). *Just left of the setting sun*. Tokyo: Blue Ocean Press.

Aguon, J. (2006). *The fire this time: Essays on life under U.S. occupation*. Tokyo: Ocean Press.

Akibayashi, K., & Takazato, S. (2009). Okinawa: Women's struggle for demilitarization. In C. Lutz (Ed.), *The bases of empire: The global struggle against U.S. military posts* (pp. 243–269). New York: NYU Press.

Aldrich, R., & Connell, J. (1998). *The last colonies*. Cambridge: Cambridge University Press.

Anderson, B. (1991). *Imagined communities*. New York: Verso.

Appadurai, A. (1996). Sovereignty without territoriality: Notes for a postnational geography. In P. Yeager (Ed.), *The geography of identity* (pp. 40–58). Ann Arbor: University of Michigan Press.

Arnold, D. (1996). *The problem of nature*. New York: Blackwell.

Atomic age: Look homeward, Angel. (1946, November 11). *Time*, p. 31.

Bacevich, A. (2003). *The imperial tense : Prospects and problems of American empire*. Chicago: Ivan Dee.

Baldacchino, G. (2010). *Island enclaves: Offshoring strategies, creative governance and subnational jurisdictions*. Montreal: McGill-Queens University Press.

Barthes, R. (1981). *Camera lucida: Reflections on photography*. New York: Hill and Wang.

Baudrillard, J. (1981). *For a critique of the political economy of the sign*. St. Louis: Telos.

Baudrillard, J. (1994). *Simulacra and simulation*. Ann Arbor: University of Michigan Press.

Becker, M. (2007, March 17). Ecuador: International Conference for the Abolition of Military Bases. *COA News*. Retrieved from http://www.coanews.org/tiki-read_article.php?articleId=1733

Benítez-Rojo, A. (1997). *The repeating island: The Caribbean and the postmodern perspective*. Durham: Duke University Press.

Bernazzoli, R., & Flint, C. (2009). Power, place, and militarism: Toward a comparative geographic analysis of militarization. *Geography Compass, 3*, 393–411.

Bevacqua, M. (2010). The exceptional life and death of a Chamorro soldier: Tracing the militarization of desire in Guam, USA. In S. Shigematsu & K. Camacho (Eds.), *Militarized currents: Towards a decolonized future in Asia and the Pacific* (pp. 33–62). Minneapolis: University of Minnesota Press.

Bloomfield, L. (2006). Politics and diplomacy of the global defense posture review. In C. Lords (Ed.), *Reposturing the force: U.S. overseas presence in the twenty-first century* (pp. 49–64). Newport: Naval War College.

Blumenthal, D., Mazza, M., Schriver, R., Stokes, M., & Russell Hsiao, L. C. (2011, August 30). *Asian alliances in the 21st century*. Retrieved January 24, 2014, from American Enterprise Institute website: http://www.aei.org/files/2011/08/30/Asian-Alliances-21st-Century.pdf

Bookchin, M. (1982). *The ecology of freedom: The emergence and dissolution of hierarchy*. Palo Alto, Calif.: Cheshire Books.

Braun, B. (2002). *The intemperate rainforest: Nature, culture, and power on Canada's west coast*. Minneapolis: University of Minnesota Press.

Breines, W. (1980). Community and organization: The new left and Michels' "Iron Law." *Social Problems, 27*(4), 419–429.

Brown, M., & Staeheli, L. (2003). "Are we there yet?" Feminist political geographies. *Gender, Place and Culture 10*, 247–255.

Burger, J. (1998). Attitudes about recreation, environmental problems, and estuarine health along the New Jersey shore, USA. *Environmental Management, 22*(6), 869–876.

Burger, J., Sanchez, J., Gibbons, J. W., & Gochfeld, M. (1997). Risk perception, federal spending, and the Savannah River Site: Attitudes of hunters and fishermen. *Risk Analysis, 17(3)*, 313–320.

Calder, K. E. (2007). *Embattled garrisons: Comparative base politics and American globalism*. Princeton: Princeton University Press.

Camacho, L. (2013). Poison in our waters: A brief overview of the proposed militarization of Guam and the Commonwealth of the Northern Mariana Islands. *The Asia-Pacific Journal, 11*(51). Retrieved December 29, 2013, from http://www.japanfocus.org/-Leevin-Camacho/4050

Cameron, J. (1970, March 1). Twenty-three nuclear explosions later. *New York Times Magazine*, p. 24+.

Campbell, D. (1996). Political prosaics, transversal politics, and the anarchical world. In M. Shapiro & H. Alker (Eds.), *Challenging boundaries: Global flow and territorial identities* (pp. 7–31). Minneapolis: University of Minnesota Press.

Casey, E. (2001). Between geography and philosophy: What does it mean to be in the place-world? *Annals of the Association of American Geographers, 91*, 683–693.

Castells, M. (1996). *Rise of the network society*. Cambridge: Blackwell.

Chang, T. C. (2000). Singapore's little India: A tourist attraction as a contested landscape. *Urban Studies, 37*(2), 343–366.

Cheong, S., & Miller, M. L. (2000). Power and tourism: A Foucauldian observation. *The Annals of Tourism Research, 27*(2), 371–390.

Chomsky, N. (1998). *Free Markets?* Video. Retrieved from http://youtu.be/WHj2GaPuEhY.

Clinton, H. (2011, November). America's Pacific century. *Foreign Policy*. Retrieved from http://www.foreignpolicy.com/articles/2011/10/11/americas_pacific_century

Cohen, C. (1995). Marketing paradise, making nation. *Annals of Tourism Research, 22*(2), 404–421.

Cole, W. (2007, January 8). More Marines bound for O'ahu, Guam. *Honolulu Advertiser*. Retrieved January 14, 2007, from http://the.honoluluadvertiser.com/article/2007/Jan/08/in/FP701080335.html

Coleman, M., & Grove, K. (2009). Biopolitics, biopower, and the return of sovereignty. *Environment and Planning D: Society and Space, 27*(3), 489.

Collier, S., & Lakoff, A. (2009). *On vital systems security*. International Affairs Working Paper 2009-01. Retrieved June 5, 2012, from http://test.gpia.info/files/u16/Collier_and_Lakoff_2009-01.pdf

Cosgrove, D. (1998). Introduction: Project plowshare. *Ecumene* 5, 263–266.

Cowen, D. (2010). A Geography of logistics: Market authority and security of supply chains. *Annals of the Association of American Geographers*, 100(3), 1–21.

Cresswell, T. (2004). *Place: A short introduction*. Malden, Mass.: Blackwell.

Critchlow, R. (2005). *U.S. military overseas basing: New developments and oversight issues for Congress*. Washington: Congressional Research Service.

Cumbers, A., Routledge, P., & Nativel, C. (2008). The entangled geographies of global justice networks. *Progress in Human Geography, 32*(2), 183–201.

Curtsinger, B. (1995, January 1). Close encounters with gray reef sharks. *National Geographic*, 45-67.

D'Arcus, B. (2000). The "eager gaze of the tourist" meets "our grandfathers' guns": Producing and contesting the land of enchantment in Gallup, New Mexico. *Environment and Planning D: Society and Space, 18*, 692–713.

Davis, J. (1994, May 1). Bikini's silver lining. *New York Times Magazine*, p. 42+.

Davis, J. S. (2005a). Representing place: "Deserted isles" and the reproduction of Bikini Atoll. *Annals of the Association of American Geographers, 95*, 607–625.

Davis, J. S. (2005b). "Is it really safe? That's what we want to know": Science, stories and dangerous places. *Professional Geographer, 57*, 213–221.

Davis, J. S. (2007a). Scales of Eden: Conservation and pristine devastation on Bikini Atoll. *Environment and Planning D: Society and Space, 25*, 213–235.

Davis, J. S. (2007b). Military natures: Militarism and the environment. *GeoJournal 69*(3), 131–134.

Davis, S. (2011). The U.S. military base network and contemporary colonialism: Power projection, resistance, and the quest for operational unilateralism. *Political Geography, 30*, 215–224.

Davis, S. (2012). Repeating islands of resistance: Redefining security in militarized landscapes. *Human Geography, 5*(1), 1–18.

Davis, S., Hayes-Conroy, J., & Jones, V. (2007). Military contamination and natural purity: Seeing nature and knowing contamination in Vieques, Puerto Rico. *Geojournal, 69*(3), 165–179.

Day, R. (2005). *Gramsci is dead: Anarchist currents in the newest social movements.* London: Pluto.

Delgado, J. (1996). *Ghost fleet: The sunken ships of Bikini Atoll.* Honolulu: University of Hawaii Press.

Delgado, J., Lenihan, D., & Murphy, L. (1991). *The archeology of the atomic bomb: A submerged cultural resources assessment of the sunken fleet of Operation Crossroads at Bikini and Kwajalein Atoll lagoons.* Santa Fe: National Park Service.

DeLoughrey, E. (2007). *Routes and roots: Navigating Caribbean and Pacific Island literatures.* Honolulu: University of Hawaii Press.

Dening, G. (1996). *Performances.* Chicago: University of Chicago Press.

DeOliver, M. (1996). Historical preservation and identity: The Alamo and the production of a consumer landscape. *Antipode, 28*(1), 1–23.

Department of Defense. (2002). *DoD environmental community involvement programs at test and training ranges.* Retrieved from http://www.dodig.mil/audit/reports/fy02/02-122.pdf

Department of Defense. (2004). Strengthening U.S. global defense posture: Report to Congress. Retrieved from http://www.dmzhawaii.org/wp-content/uploads/2008/12/global_posture.pdf

Department of Defense. (2010). *2010 quadrennial defense review.* Retrieved from http://www.defense.gov/qdr/images/QDR_as_of_12Feb10_1000.pdf

Desmond, J. (1999). *Staging tourism.* Chicago: University of Chicago Press.

Diggs, F. (1969, October 13). Reclaiming the world's most H-bombed area. *U.S. News and World Report, 67,* 98–101.

Dowler, L., Carubia, J., & Szcygiel, B. (2005). *Gender and landscape.* New York: Routledge.

Dowler, L., & Sharp, J. (2001). A feminist geopolitics? *Space and Polity,* 5, 165–176.

Doyle, D. (2005). "The salt water washes away all impropriety": Mass culture and the middle class body on the beach in turn of the century Atlantic City. In L. Dowler, J. Carubia, & B. Szczygiel (Eds.), *Gender and Landscape* (pp. ???). New York: Routledge.

Duncan, J., & Duncan, N. (2001). The aestheticization of the politics of landscape preservation. *Annals of the Association of American Geographers, 91,* 387–409.

Duncan, J., & Ley, D. (Eds.). (1993). *Place/culture/representation.* New York: Routledge.

Dunn, G. (1996). The people of tourist brochures. In T. Selwyn (Ed.), *The tourist image: Myths and myth making in tourism* (pp. 61–82). New York: Wiley and Sons.

Echtner, C., & Prasad, P. (2003). The context of third world tourism marketing. *Annals of Tourism Research, 30*(3), 660–682.

Edensor, T. (1998). *Tourists at the Taj: Performance and meaning at a symbolic site*. New York: Routledge.

Enloe, C. (1990). *Bananas, beaches, & bases: Making feminist sense of international politics*. Berkeley: University of California Press.

Enloe, C. (2000). *Maneuvers: The international politics of militarizing women's lives*. Berkeley: University of California Press.

Enloe, C. (2007). *Globalization and militarism: Feminists make the link*. New York: Rowman & Littlefield.

Erickson, A., & Mikolay, J. (2006). A place and a base: Guam and the American presence in East Asia. In C. Lords (Ed.), *Reposturing the force: U.S. overseas presence in the twenty-first century* (pp. 65–94). Newport: Naval War College.

Evans, J., & Hall, S. (1999). *Visual culture: The reader*. London: Sage.

Ferguson, K., & Turnbull, P. (1998). *Oh, say, can you see: The semiotics of the military in Hawai'i*. Minneapolis: University of Minnesota Press.

Flint, C. (2003). Political geography: Context and agency in a multiscalar framework. *Progress in Human Geography, 27*, 627–636.

Fluri, J. (2006). "Our website was revolutionary": Virtual spaces of representation and resistance. *ACME, 5*, 89–111.

Fluri, J. (2012). Capitalizing on bare life: Sovereignty, exception, and gender politics. *Antipode, 44*(1), 31–50.

Foucault, M. (1980). *Power/knowledge: Selected interviews and other writings, 1972–1977*. New York: Random House.

Foucault, M. (2003). *"Society must be defended": Lectures at the Collège de France, 1975–1976*. New York: Macmillan.

Foucault, M. (2007). *Security, territory, population: Lectures at the Collège de France, 1977–1978*. New York: Palgrave Macmillan.

French, H. (2001, June 11). Dark side of U.S. quest for security: Squalor on an atoll. *New York Times*. Retrieved from http://www.nytimes.com/2001/06/11/world/11ISLA.html?ex=1224302400&en=bf599b703a347053&ei=5070

Garamone, J. (2005). U.S. military footprint in Europe changing to meet strategy. Retrieved March 21, 2007, from http://www.defenselink.mil/news/newsarticle.aspx?id=31251

Ge, S. (2003). The discussion of Asia and our predicament. *Sungkyun Journal of East Asian Studies, 3*(1), 31–44.

Gerson, J., & Birchard, B. (1991). *The sun never sets: Confronting the network of foreign U.S. military bases*. Boston: South End Press.

Gibson-Graham, J-K. (2008). Diverse economies: Performative practices for "other worlds." *Progress in Human Geography, 32*, 613–632.

Gillem, M. (2007). *America town: Building the outposts of empire*. Minneapolis: University of Minnesota Press.

Glassman, J. (2001). From Seattle (and Ubon) to Bangkok: The scales of resistance to corporate globalization. *Environment and Planning D: Society and Space, 19*, 513–533.

Glassman, J. (2005). The new imperialism? On continuity and change in U.S. foreign policy. *Environment and Planning A, 37*, 1527–1544.

Gonzalez, V. (2013). *Securing paradise: Tourism and militarism in Hawaii and the Philippines*. Durham: Duke University Press.

Gramsci, A. (1971). *Prison notebooks*. New York: International Publishers.

Greenberg, M. (1997). Bombs and butterflies: A case study of the challenges of post cold war environmental planning and management for the U.S. nuclear weapons sites. *Journal of Environmental Planning and Management, 40*, 739–750.

Gregory, D. (2004). *The colonial present*. Cambridge, Mass.: Blackwell.

Gregory, D., & Pred, A. (2007). *Violent geographies: Fear, terror and political violence*. New York: Routledge.

Grossman, Z. (2002). New U.S. military bases: Side effects or causes of war? *Counterpunch*. Retrieved August 4, 2006, from http:www.counterpunch.com.org/zoltanbases.html

Grove, R. (1995). *Green Imperialism*. Cambridge: Cambridge University Press.

Grugel, J. (2004). State power and transnational activism. In N. Piper & A. Uhlin (Eds.), *Transnational activism in Asia: Problems of power and democracy* (Vol. 13, pp. 26–42). New York: Routledge.

Guthrie, D. (2008). *China and globalization: The social, economic and political transformation of Chinese society*. New York: Routledge.

Hall, T. (1997). Images of industry in the post-industrial city: Raymond Mason and Birmingham. *Ecumene, 4*(1), 46–68.

Hannah, M. (2006). Torture and the ticking bomb: The war on terrorism as a geographical imagination of power/knowledge. *Annals of the Association of American Geographers, 96*, 622–640.

Haraway, D. (1997). *Modest_Witness@Second_Millennium: FemaleMan©Meets_OncoMouseTM*. London: Routledge.

Hardt, M., & Negri, A. (2000). *Empire*. Cambridge, Mass.: Harvard University Press.

Hardt, M., & Negri, A. (2004). *Multitude: War and democracy in the age of empire*. Chicago: Penguin.

Harvey, D. (1990). *The condition of postmodernity*. Cambridge: Blackwell.

Harvey, D. (1996). *Justice, nature and the geography of difference*. Cambridge: Blackwell.

Harvey, D. (2003). *The new imperialism*. Oxford: Oxford Press.

Harvey, D. (2005). *A brief history of neoliberalism*. Oxford: Oxford Press.

Hau'ofa, E. (1994). *Our sea of islands. The Contemporary Pacific, 6*, 148–161.

Havlick, D. (2007). Logics of change for military-to-wildlife conversions in the United States. *GeoJournal, 9*(3), 145–164.

Hayes-Conroy, J. (2008). Hope for community? Anarchism, exclusion, and the nonhuman realm. *Political Geography, 27*, 29–34.

Hayes-Conroy, J., & Hayes-Conroy, A. (2013). Veggies and visceralities: A political ecology of food and feeling. *Emotion, Space, and Society, 6*, pp. 81–90.

Heaney, T. (2005). How to travel with a male. In L. Dowler, J. Carubia, & B. Szczygiel (Eds.), *Gender and Landscape (pp. 109–123).* New York: Routledge.

Henry, R. (2006). Transforming the U.S. global defense posture. In C. Lords (Ed.), *Reposturing the force: U.S. overseas presence in the twenty-first century* (pp. 33–48). Newport: Naval War College.

Hentz, J. (2004). *The obligation of empire: United States' grand strategy for a new century.* Lexington: University of Kentucky Press.

Herb, G. (2005). The geography of peace movements. In C. Flint (Ed.), *The geography of war and peace* (pp. 347–368). Oxford: Oxford University Press.

Herman, R. (2008). Inscribing empire: Guam and the war in the Pacific National Historical Park. *Political Geography, 27*, 630–651.

Herod, A., & Wright, M. (2002). *Geographies of power: Placing scale.* Malden, Mass.: Blackwell.

Hezel, F. (1995). *Strangers in their own land: A century of colonial rule in the Caroline and Marshall Islands.* Honolulu: University of Hawai'i Press.

Hoelscher, S. (1998). Tourism, ethnic memory and the other-directed place. E*cumene,* 5(4), 369–398.

Holloway, J. (2002). *Change the world without taking power.* London: Pluto.

Howe, K. (2000). *The knowing of Oceania.* Honolulu: University of Hawai'i Press.

Hutt, M. (1996). Looking for Shangri-la: From Hilton to Lamichhane. In T. Selwyn (Ed.), *The tourist image: Myths and myth making in tourism* (pp. 49–60). New York: Wiley and Sons.

Hyndman, J. (2004). Mind the gap: Bridging feminist and political geography through geopolitics. *Political Geography, 23*, 307–322.

Inoue, M. (2004). We are Okinawans but of a different kind. *Current Anthropology, 45*, 85–104.

Intellectuals in Okinawa assert that the Senkaku Islands should be shared. (2013, January 17). Ryukyu Shimpo. Retrieved January 27, 2014, from http://english.ryukyushimpo.jp/2013/01/17/9033/

Ireland, B. (2010). *The U.S. military in Hawai'i: Colonialism, memory and resistance.* New York: Palgrave Macmillan.

Jackson, J. B. (1994). *A sense of place, a sense of time.* New Haven, Conn.: Yale University Press.

Jackson, P. (1989). *Maps of meaning.* New York: Routledge.

Johnson, C. (2004). *The sorrows of empire: Militarism, secrecy, and the end of the republic.* New York: Metropolitan Books.

Johnson, C. (2007). *Nemesis: The last days of the American republic.* New York: Metropolitan Books.

Johnson, G. (1980). Nuclear legacy: Islands laid waste. *Oceans, 13*, 57–60.

Jolly, M. (1997). From Point Venus to Bali Ha'i: Eroticism and exoticism in representations of the Pacific. In L. Manderson & M. Jolly (Eds.), *Sites of desire, economies of pleasure* (pp. 99–122).. Chicago: University of Chicago Press.

Jones, L., & Sage, D. (2010). New directions in critical geopolitics: An introduction. *Geojournal, 75*, 315–325.

Jones, R. (2012). *Border walls: Security and the war on terror in the United States, India, and Israel.* London: Zed Books.

Kaplan, R. (2005, June). How we would fight China. *The Atlantic*. Retrieved December 27, 2013, from http://www.theatlantic.com/magazine/archive/2005/06/how-we-would-fight-china/3959/

Karatani, K. (2008). Beyond capital-nation-state. *Rethinking Marxism, 20*(4), 569–595.

Katsiaficas, G. N. (1987). *The imagination of the New Left: A global analysis of 1968.* Boston: South End Press.

Kearns, G. (2004). The political pivot of geography. *Geographical Journal, 170*(4), 337–346.

Kennedy, P. (1987). *The rise and fall of the great powers: Economic change and military conflict from 1500 to 2000.* London: Fontana.

Kirk, G. (2008, March 14). Gender and U.S. bases in Asia-Pacific. *Foreign Policy in Focus.*

Kirsch, S. (1997). Watching the bombs go off: Photography, nuclear landscapes and spectator democracy. *Antipode, 29*, 227–255.

Kirsch, S. (2007). Ecologists and the experimental landscape: The nature of science at the U.S. Department of Energy's Savannah River Site. *Cultural Geographies, 14*(4), 485–510.

Kiste, R. (1974). *The Bikinians: A study in forced migration.* Menlo Park, Calif.: Cummings.

Kiste, R. (1985). Identity and relocation: The Bikini case. *Pacific Viewpoint, 26*(1), 116–138.

Klein, N. (2007). *The shock doctrine: The rise of disaster capitalism.* New York: Picador / Henry Holt and Company.

Koopman, S. (2011). Alter-geopolitics: Other securities are happening. *Geoforum, 42*(3), 274–284.

Kristof, N. (1997, March 5). An atomic age Eden (but don't eat the coconuts). *New York Times*, Sec. A, p. 4, c. 3.

Kropotkin, P. (1885). What geography ought to be. *Nineteenth Century*, 18, 940–56.

Krupar, S. (2007). Where eagles dare: An ethno-fable with personal landfill. *Environment and Planning D: Society and Space, 25*, 194–212.

Krygier, J. (1998). Project Ketch: Project Plowshare in Pennsylvania. *Ecumene, 5*, 311–322.

Larsen, S., & Johnson, J. (2012). Toward an open sense of place: Phenomenology, affinity, and the question of being. *Annals of the Association of American Geographers, 102*(3), 632–646.

Latour, B. (1993). *We have never been modern.* Cambridge: Harvard University Press.

Lefebvre, H. (1991). *The production of space.* Cambridge: Blackwell.

Lemke, T. (2005). "A zone of indistinction": A critique of Giorgio Agamben's concept of biopolitics. *Outlines: Critical Practice Studies, 7*(1), 3–13.

Lilomaiava-Doktor, S. (2009). Beyond "migration": Samoan population movement (Malaga) and the geography of social space (Va). *Contemporary Pacific, 21*(1), 1–32.

Lords, C. (2006). Introduction. In C. Lords (Ed.), *Reposturing the force: U.S. overseas presence in the twenty-first century* (pp. 1–8). Newport: Naval War College.

Loyd, J. M., Mitchelson, M., & Burridge, A. (2012). *Beyond walls and cages: Prisons, borders, and global crisis.* Athens: University of Georgia Press.

Lutz, C. (2001). *Homefront.* Boston: Beacon Press.

Lutz, C. (2002). Making war at home in the United States: Militarization and the current crisis. *American Anthropologist, 104*, 723–735.

Lutz, C. (2006). Empire is in the details. *American Ethnologist, 33*(4), 593–611.

Lutz, C. (2009). *The bases of empire: The global struggle against U.S. military posts.* New York: NYU Press.

Lutz, C., & Collins, J. (1993). *Reading National Geographic.* Chicago: University of Chicago Press.

MacCormack, C., & Strathern, M. (1980). *Nature, culture and gender.* Cambridge: Cambridge University Press.

MacDougall, W. (1974, December 16). Twenty-eight years after atom blast: The Bikinians return home. *U.S. News and World Report, 77*, 52–54.

Mackinder, H. (1904). The geographic pivot of history. *Geographical Journal, 23*, 421–37.

Markwith, C. (1946, July). Farewell to Bikini. *National Geographic, 90*, 97–116.

Marston, S. (2000). The social construction of scale. *Progress in Human Geography, 24*, 219–242.

Massey, D. (1991). Flexible sexism. *Environment and Planning D: Society and Space, 9*, 31–57.

Massey, D. (1994). *Space, place and gender.* Minneapolis: University of Minnesota Press.

Massey, D. (2004). Geographies of responsibility. *Geografiska Annaler*: Series B, *Human Geography, 86*(1), 5–18.

Matthews, L. (2010, October 22). Proposed firing ranges will have no explosives. *Pacific Daily News.*

Mbembé, J.-A. (2003). Necropolitics. *Public Culture, 15*(1), 11–40.

McCaffrey, K. (2002). *Military power and popular protest: The U.S. Navy in Vieques, Puerto Rico.* New Brunswick, N.J.: Rutgers University Press.

McCarthy, J. (2005). Scale, sovereignty, and strategy in environmental governance. *Antipode, 37*, 731–753.

McCormack, G., & Norimatsu, S. (2012). *Resistant islands: Okinawa confronts Japan and the United States.* New York: Rowman & Littlefield.

McGuirk, P. M., & Rowe, D. (2001). "Defining moments" and refining myths in the making of place identity: The Newcastle Knights and the Australian Rugby League grand final. *Australian Geographical Studies, 39*(1):52–66.

Merchant, C. (2004). *Reinventing Eden: The fate of nature in Western culture.* New York: Routledge.

Minca, C. (2006). Giorgio Agamben and the new biopolitical *nomos. Geografiska Annaler*: Series B, *Human Geography, 88*(4), 387–403.

Minca, C. (2007). Agamben's geographies of modernity. *Political Geography, 26*(1), 78–97.

Misrach, R. (1990). *Bravo 20: The bombing of the American West.* Baltimore: Johns Hopkins Press.

Morehouse, B. (2004). Theoretical approaches to border spaces and identities. In V. Pavlakovich-Kochi, B. Morehouse, & D. Wastl-Walter (Eds.), *Challenged borderlands: Transcending political and cultural boundaries* (pp. 19–40). Burlington, Vt.: Ashgate.

Mydans, C. (1968, October 18). Twenty-two years—twenty-three blasts later: Return to Bikini. *Life, 65*, 28–37.

Natividad, L., & Kirk, G. (2010, May 10). Fortress Guam: Resistance to U.S. military mega-buildup. *Asia-Pacific Journal.*

Neumann, R. (1998). *Imposing wilderness: Struggles over livelihood and nature preservation in Africa.* Berkeley: University of California Press.

Neumann, R. (2003). The production of nature: Colonial recasting of the African landscape in Serengeti National Park. In K. Zimmerer & T Bassett (Eds.), *Political ecology: An integrative approach to geography and environment-development studies* (pp. 240–255). New York: Guilford Press.

Niedenthal, J. (1997). A history of the people of Bikini following nuclear weapons testing in the Marshall Islands: With recollections and views of elders of Bikini Atoll. *Health Physics, 73*, 28–36.

Niedenthal, J. (2001). *For the good of mankind: A history of the people of Bikini and their islands.* Majuro, Marshall Islands: Bravo.

Oakes, T. (1997). Place and the paradox of modernity. *Annals of the Association of American Geographers, 87*, 509–531.

Osorio, J. (2010). Memorializing Pu'uloa and remembering Pearl Harbor. In S. Shigematsu & Keith Camacho (Eds.), *Militarized currents: Toward a decolonized future in Asia and the Pacific* (pp. 1–14). Minneapolis: University of Minnesota Press.

Ó Tuathail, G. (1996). An anti-geopolitical eye: Maggie O'Kane in Bosnia, 1992–93. *Gender, Place and Culture, 3*, 171–185.

Ó Tuathail, G., & Dalby, S. (1998). *Rethinking geopolitics: Towards a critical geopolitics.* New York: Routledge.

Peña, D. (1997). *The terror of the machine: Technology, work, gender, and ecology on the U.S.-Mexico border.* Austin: University of Texas Press.

Petersen, G. (1998). Strategic location and sovereignty: Modern Micronesia in the historical context of American expansionism. *Space and Polity, 2*, 179–205.

Pilger, J. (1989). *The secret country.* New York: Knopf.

Pincas, W. (1975, May 17). Bikini and Eniwetok: Repaying old debts. *New Republic*, pp. 11–14.

Posen, B. (2003). Command of the commons: The military foundation of U.S. hegemony. *International Security, 28*(1), 5–46.

Poyer, L., Falgout, S., & Carucci, L. (2001). *The typhoon of war: Micronesian experiences of the Pacific War.* Honolulu: University of Hawai'i Press.

Pratt, M. L. (1992). *Imperial eyes: Travel writing and transculturation.* New York: Routledge.

Pratt, W. (1946, February 18). How Bikini became the bomb-testing ground. *Newsweek, 27,* 60.

Robbins, P. (2012). *Political ecology: A critical introduction.* Malden, Mass.: Blackwell.

Robinson, F. (1999). *Globalizing care: Ethics, feminist theory, and international relations.* Boulder: Westview Press.

Rogers, R. (1994). *Destiny's landfall: A history of Guam.* Honolulu: University of Hawai'i Press.

Rooney, E. (1946, March 31). The strange people from Bikini: Primitive they are, but they love one another and the American visitors who took their home. *New York Times Magazine,* p. 23+.

Rose, G. (2001). *Visual methodologies: An introduction to the interpretation of visual materials.* London: Sage.

Said, E. (1979). *Orientalism.* New York: Vintage.

Sandars, C. (2000). *America's overseas garrisons: The leasehold empire.* Oxford: Oxford University Press.

Santana, D. (2006). La lucha continúa: Challenges for a post-navy Vieques. *CENTRO, 18,* 108–123.

Satoko, N. (2011, February 28). Hatoyama's confession: The myth of deterrence and the failure to move a Marine base outside Okinawa. *Asia-Pacific Journal, 9*(9), no. 3, 2.

Schweller, R., & Pu, X. (2011). After unipolarity: China's visions of international order in an era of U.S. decline. *International Security, 36*(1), 41–72.

Scott, J. (1999). *Seeing like a state: How certain schemes to improve the human condition have failed.* New Haven, Conn.: Yale.

Scott, J. (2009). *The art of not being governed: An anarchist history of upland Southeast Asia.* New Haven, Conn.: Yale.

Seager, J. (1993). *Earth follies: Coming to feminist terms with the global environmental crisis.* New York: Routledge.

Shields, R. (1991). *Places on the margin: Alternative geographies of modernity.* New York: Routledge.

Shigematsu, S., & Camacho, K. (2010). *Militarized currents: Towards a decolonized future in Asia and the Pacific.* Minneapolis: University of Minnesota Press.

Simon, S. (1997). A brief history of people and events related to atomic testing in the Marshall Islands. *Health Physics, 73,* 5–20.

Sjoberg, L. (2008). Scaling IR theory: Geography's contribution to where IR takes place. *International Studies Review, 10,* 472–500.

Smith, B. (1960). *European vision and the South Pacific, 1768–1850: A study in the history of art and ideas.* Oxford: Clarendon Press.

Smith, B. (1992). *Imagining the Pacific in the wake of the Cook voyages.* New Haven, Conn.: Yale University Press.

Smith, N. (1984). *Uneven development: Nature, capital, and the production of space.* New York: Basil Blackwell.

Smith, N. (2003). *American empire: Roosevelt's geographer and the prelude to globalization*. Berkeley: University of California Press.

Soja, E. (1996). *Thirdspace: Journeys to Los Angeles and other real-and-imagined places*. Malden, Mass.: Blackwell.

Stasch, A. D. (2006). Arc Ecology v. United States Department of the Air Force: Extending the extraterritorial reach of domestic environmental law. *Environmental Law, 36*, 1065.

Steinberg, P. (2001). *The social construction of the ocean*. Cambridge: Cambridge University Press.

Stone, R. Producer.(1988). *Radio Bikini* (Film).

Sylvester, C. (2006). Bare life as a development/postcolonial problematic. *Geographical Journal, 172*(1), 66–77.

Taussig, M. (2000). The beach (a fantasy). *Critical Inquiry, 26*, 249–278.

Teaiwa, T. (2000). Bikinis and other s/pacific n/oceans. In D. Hanlon & G. White (Eds.), *Voyaging through the contemporary Pacific* (pp. 91–112). New York: Rowman & Littlefield.

Thrift, N. (1995). A hyperactive world. In R. Johnston, P. Taylor, & M. Watts (Eds.), *Geographies of global change: Remapping the world in the late twentieth century* (pp. 18–35). Oxford: Blackwell.

Trumball, R. (1982, October 18). An island people still exiled by nuclear age. *U.S. News and World Report, 93*, 48–50.

Turner, L., & Ash, J. (1976). *The golden hordes*. New York: St. Martin's.

Ueunten, W. (2010). Rising up from a sea of discontent: The 1970 Koza uprising in U.S.-occupied Okinawa. In S. Shigematsu & K. Camacho (Eds.), *Militarized currents: Towards a decolonized Future in Asia and the Pacific* (pp. 91–124). Minneapolis: University of Minnesota Press.

Urry, J. (1990). *The tourist gaze: Leisure and travel in contemporary societies*. London: Sage.

Vine, D. (2004). War and forced migration in the Indian Ocean: The U.S. military base at Diego Garcia. *International Migration, 42*, 111–143.

Vine, D. (2009). *Island of shame: The secret history of the U.S. military base on Diego Garcia*. Princeton: Princeton University Press.

Vine, D. (2012, July 15). U.S. empire of bases grows. Tomgram posted on *TomDispatch.com*. Retrieved from http://www.tomdispatch.com/archive/175568/

Waitt, G., & Head, L. (2002). Postcards and frontier mythologies: Sustaining views of the Kimberley as timeless. *Environment and Planning D: Society and Space, 20*(3), 319–344.

Walker, R. (1993). *Inside/outside: International relations as political theory*. Cambridge: Cambridge University Press.

Wallerstein, I. (1999). *The end of the world as we know it*. Minneapolis: University of Minnesota Press.

Warf, B. (1997). The geopolitics/geoeconomics of military base closures in the USA. *Political Geography, 16*, 541–563.

Weaver, T. (2010, March 5). Guam expansion central to U.S. realignment strategy in Asia. *Stars and Stripes.* Retrieved from http://www.stripes.com/news/guam-expansion-central-to-u-s-realignment-strategy-in-asia-1.99723

Weideman, E. (1954, October 9). Ashes of death: First H-bomb victims. *Nation, 179,* 328–9.

Weisgall, J. (1980). The nuclear nomads of Bikini. *Foreign Policy, 39,* 74–98.

Weisgall, J. (1994). *Operation Crossroads: The atomic tests at Bikini Atoll.* Annapolis, Md.: Naval Institute Press.

Wilson, R. (2000). *Reimagining the American Pacific: From* South Pacific *to Bamboo Ridge and beyond.* Durham: Duke University Press.

Women for Genuine Security. (2011). What is genuine security? Retrieved March 23, 2011, from http://www.genuinesecurity.org/aboutus/whatisGS.html

Woodward, R. (2004). *Military geographies.* Malden, Mass.: Blackwell.

Woodward, R. (2005). From military geography to militarism's geographies: Disciplinary engagements with the geographies of militarism and military activities. *Progress in Human Geography, 6,* 718–740.

Wright, M. (2006). *Disposable women and other myths of global capitalism.* New York: Routledge.

Yapa, L. (1996). Improved seeds and constructed scarcity. In R. Peet & M. Watts (Eds.), *Liberation ecologies: Environment, development, and social movements* (pp. 69–85). New York: Routledge.

Zielinski, D. (2009). *No virtue like efficacy: Considering Guam's operational vulnerabilities.* Newport, R.I.: Naval War College.

INDEX

GEOGRAPHIES OF JUSTICE AND SOCIAL TRANSFORMATION

1. *Social Justice and the City*, rev. ed.
BY DAVID HARVEY
2. *Begging as a Path to Progress: Indigenous Women and Children and the Struggle for Ecuador's Urban Spaces*
BY KATE SWANSON
3. *Making the San Fernando Valley: Rural Landscapes, Urban Development, and White Privilege*
BY LAURA R. BARRACLOUGH
4. *Company Towns in the Americas: Landscape, Power, and Working-Class Communities*
EDITED BY OLIVER J. DINIUS AND ANGELA VERGARA
5. *Tremé: Race and Place in a New Orleans Neighborhood*
BY MICHAEL E. CRUTCHER JR.
6. *Bloomberg's New York: Class and Governance in the Luxury City*
BY JULIAN BRASH
7. *Roppongi Crossing: The Demise of a Tokyo Nightclub District and the Reshaping of a Global City*
BY ROMAN ADRIAN CYBRIWSKY
8. *Fitzgerald: Geography of a Revolution*
BY WILLIAM BUNGE
9. *Accumulating Insecurity: Violence and Dispossession in the Making of Everyday Life*
EDITED BY SHELLEY FELDMAN, CHARLES GEISLER, AND GAYATRI A. MENON
10. *They Saved the Crops: Labor, Landscape, and the Struggle over Industrial Farming in Bracero-Era California*
BY DON MITCHELL
11. *Faith Based: Religious Neoliberalism and the Politics of Welfare in the United States*
BY JASON HACKWORTH
12. *Fields and Streams: Stream Restoration, Neoliberalism, and the Future of Environmental Science*
BY REBECCA LAVE

13. *Black, White, and Green: Farmers Markets, Race, and the Green Economy*
BY ALISON HOPE ALKON

14. *Beyond Walls and Cages: Prisons, Borders, and Global Crisis*
EDITED BY JENNA M. LOYD, MATT MITCHELSON, AND ANDREW BURRIDGE

15. *Silent Violence: Food, Famine, and Peasantry in Northern Nigeria*
BY MICHAEL J. WATTS

16. *Development, Security, and Aid: Geopolitics and Geoeconomics at the U.S. Agency for International Development*
BY JAMEY ESSEX

17. *Properties of Violence: Law and Land-Grant Struggle in Northern New Mexico*
BY DAVID CORREIA

18. *Geographical Diversions: Tibetan Trade, Global Transactions*
BY TINA HARRIS

19. *The Politics of the Encounter: Urban Theory and Protest under Planetary Urbanization*
BY ANDY MERRIFIELD

20. *Rethinking the South African Crisis: Nationalism, Populism, Hegemony*
BY GILLIAN HART

21. *The Empires' Edge: Militarization, Resistance, and Transcending Hegemony in the Pacific*
BY SASHA DAVIS